ميدو

© 2017 by Matthew Aldrich

The author's moral rights have been asserted. All rights reserved. No part of this document may be reproduced or transmitted in any form or by any means, electronic, mechanical, photocopying, recording, or otherwise, without prior written permission of the publisher.

ISBN: 978-0998641119

Conceptualized and edited by Matthew Aldrich

Written by Mariam Khaled

Illustrated by Mona Mohamed

Photographs by Remon Maher

Audio by Mohamed Ibrahim and Amel Shafii

website: www.lingualism.com

email: contact@lingualism.com

Table of Contents

2 .... Introduction

3 .... Orthography

الفصْل الاوّل: عيْلِة ميدو 4

الفصْل التاني: المحطّه الخاطِئه 18

الفصْل التّالِت: زِيارِة تيْته 32

الفصْل الرّابِع: المعاد السِّرّي 48

الفصْل الخامِس: تزْويغ عمْرو 62

الفصْل السّادِس: صديق ميدو السِّرّي 76

الفصْل السّابِع: الازْمه 96

الفصْل التّامِن: كُبّايِة شاي عِنْد الجيران 112

الفصْل التّاسِع: محفْظِة الاحْلام 128

الفصْل العاشِر: مخْطوف 146

Supplementary materials for Mido in Egyptian Arabic are available at **www.lingualism.com/mido-ea**:

- Free audio files
- Free PDF with page-by-page vocabulary lists and an alphabetical glossary
- Anki flashcards with audio (available separately)

Introduction

I remember with great fondness reading *Le Petit Nicolas* stories in college. Childlike in their innocence, they were a welcome break from the more serious literature in the syllabus. This inspired me to create *Mido* for Arabic students.

The stories in this book are light-hearted and easy to follow, but also engaging, all the while presenting the lively language and culture of Egyptians today. However, these stories are aimed at adult language-learners—and not children—as secrets and lies and crime make appearances.

The first chapter serves as an introduction to Mido and his family, as we take a peek at the household's typical morning. Mido's father, mother, brother, and sister each feature in a chapter showing a day in their lives. And Mido, our hero, stars in the remaining chapters.

The Egyptian Arabic texts appear on the left-facing pages, while the English translations can be found on the right-facing pages along with cultural and language notes, as well as photographs.

Dozens of beautiful illustrations can be found throughout the book to help the reader better understand the texts. Audio professionally recorded by voice actors in Cairo is available to stream or download for free from: **www.lingualism.com/mido-ea**

I would like to thank Mona Mohamed, Mohamed Ibrahim, Amel Shafii, and Remon Maher for their contributions to this project. And I wish to extend a special thank-you to Mariam Khaled, who listened to my ideas about Mido and his family's adventures and turned them into the wonderful, vivid stories in this book, which would never have been possible without her creativity and hard work. Thank you, Mariam!

I hope you enjoy *Mido* and learn more Egyptian Arabic along the way.

Matthew Aldrich

Orthography

There is no official system of spelling Egyptian Colloquial Arabic. There are many conventions used by the majority of Egyptians, but individual preferences abound. The official, written language is, of course, Modern Standard Arabic. But when Egyptians do write in their dialect, they tend to follow orthographic rules of MSA to a point, while sounding things out and spelling them as they see fit when in doubt.

In *Lingualism* publications, every effort has been made to standardize the spelling for consistency, using some of the most common spelling preferences among Egyptians. This includes omitting dots from final *yaa* (ى instead of ي) and *taa marbuta* (ه instead of ة). ة is only written when in an *idaafa* construct, being pronounced *t*.

The texts contain *tashkeel* (diacritics) to assist in reading. *Kasra* (ِ) and *damma* (ُ) are written to mark short vowels. They are not written before the long vowels *yaa* and *waw*.

Sukuun (ْ) is not written word-final to avoid cluttering the text, as Egyptian Arabic does not have case endings (*i3raab*). *Sukuun* is written over *waw* when pronounced *ō* and over *yaa* when pronounced *ē:* يوْم (*yōm* day), بيْت (*bēt* house).

Fatha, the most common vowel in Arabic, is not normally written, in order to avoid clutter, as well. When a consonant is not marked, the default vowel is *fatha*. It is, however, written above an initial *waw* or *yaa*, and in a few other cases, for clarity. It is also written before *waw* and *yaa* when they are pronounced as diphthongs: هَيْكون (*haykūn* will be), مَوْجود (*mawgūd* present).

Kasra is not written in the definite article ال. The word اللي (*illi*) is written without *kasra* and *sukuun*.

The PDF eBook version of this book, available at **www.lingualism.com/mido-ea** includes an unvoweled version for those who prefer reading without *tashkeel*.

الفصْل الاوّل: عيْلةِ ميدو

"ميدو! اِنْتَ يا واد يا ميدو! اِصْحَى! طابور المدْرسه هَيْفوتك يا وَله!"

صوْت أُمّ عمْرو و هيَّ بتْصحَّى ميدو للمدْرسه هُوّ زَيّ نشيد الصّباح اَوْ الموسيقَى التّصْويريه بِتاعِة كُلّ يوْم فى بيْت عيْلةِ ميدو و يمْكِن فى كُلّ البيوت.

ابو عمْرو صحى علَى الصّوْت طبْعاً و بعصبيه قال: "**الزّفْت** ده لِسّه مِش عاوِز يقوم!" ميدو سِمِع خطَوات ابوه الغضْبانه بتْقرّب مِن الاوْضه، راح نطّ مِن السِّرير بِسُرْعه و قال:
—انا صِحيت اهو يا بابا خلاص.
—قوم يَلّا **يا فالح** بدل ما يِقْفِلوا باب المدْرسه*.

Chapter 1: **Mido's Family**

"Mido! Come on, Mido! Wake up! You're going to miss the morning assembly at school!"

The voice of Om Amr calling for Mido to wake up is like a daily morning anthem or a soundtrack in Mido's family's house and probably in every house.

Abu Amr woke up because of the noise. Annoyed, he said, "That stupid boy is still sleeping?" As soon as Mido heard his father's angry footsteps approaching, he jumped out of bed and nervously said,

"I'm up, dad!"

"Hurry up before the school doors close."

يا واد = يا وّله = يا وَلد *hey boy!*

طابور المدْرسه (lit. *school line-up*) is the morning assembly that begins each school day in Egypt. Students line up in the school yard for the national anthem and physical exercise.

زِفْت (lit. *asphalt, tar;* here: used as an insult) *idiot, bastard*

يا فالح (sarcastic) *wise guy!*

*The school door is normally locked fifteen minutes after the start of the first class, after which students must wait until the next period to enter.

بصّ ميدو لِاخوه **عَمْرو** الكِبير، الوَلَد الاكْبَر فى العِيْله (اللى بِيتْنادَى لِابوه و مامْتُه بِاسْمُه "أُمّ عَمْرو" و "ابو عَمْرو"*) اللى كان نايِم فى السَّرير و محدِّش بيصحِّيه بدْرى زَيُّه عشان هُوَّ بيصْحى مِتأخَّر و مدْرِسْتُه الثّانويه مُمْكِن يِفْضل الباب مفتوح لحدّ السّاعه ٩، مِش ٧ و نُصّ زَيُّه.

عَمْرو كمان مُمْكِن يِخْتار يِروح أوْ يِغيب براحْتُه. ميدو فكَّر: "اِمْتَى هكْبَر زَىّ عَمْرو و اعْمِل اللى انا عاوْزُه؟"

قطع صوْت افْكارُه، صوْت مامْتُه و هِيَّ بتْنادى:

—يا ميدو يَلَّا عشان تِلْحق تِفْطر يا حبيبى. انا عمِلْتِلك سنْدويتْشينْ جِبْنه **نِسْتو** و واحِد مُربَّى و واحِد **حلاوَه**.

راح ميدو لِبِس هِدوم المدْرسه الكُحْلى معَ القميص الابْيض المِخطَّط و طِلِع عشان يِفْطر.

—حطِّيْت كُلّ كُتُبك و كراريسك اللى مِحْتاجْها فى الشِّنْطه؟ **اوْعَى** تِكون نِسيت حاجه؟

—لا يا ماما، متْخافيش. حطِّيْت كُلّ حاجه.

—يَلَّا خُد رغيف عيْش و كل مِن الطَّعْميه السُّخْنه و البطاطِس المُحمَّره اللى عامْلاها عشانك.

Mido looked at his elder brother, Amr, the eldest son in the family (and that's why his parents are called "Abu Amr" and "Om Amr"). He was still asleep in bed without anyone waking him up early. That's because he can wake up late as his high school leaves the door open until 9 a.m., and not 7:30 like his.

Amr also gets to choose whether he wants to go or not. Mido thought to himself, "When will I grow up like Amr and do what I want."

A voice interrupted his thoughts, his mother's voice, as she called, "Mido! Hurry so you have time to eat breakfast. I made you two Nesto cheese sandwiches, one jam sandwich, and one halva sandwich".

Mido put on his navy-blue school uniform, with a white striped shirt, and went to eat breakfast.

"Have you put all you books and notebooks you need in your bag? Careful not to forget anything."

"Don't worry, mom. I got everything."

"Here. Take this loaf of bread and eat the hot falafel and French fries I made for you."

عَمْرو - Notice that the final و in the name عَمْرو *Amr* is silent, but it helps distinguish it from another common name, عُمَر *Omar*.

*Such names are كُنْيَة (teknonyms), whereby parents are informally known by the name of their eldest son, or, in the absence of a son, their eldest daughter.

سَبْعه = ۷; تِسْعه = ۹

نِسْتو *Nesto* is a spreadable processed cheese sold in small, foil-wrapped wedges. It was a popular brand in the 1960s, but the name continues to be used for all such cheese. The most popular brand nowadays is البقرة الضاحكة *The Laughing Cow (La Vache Qui Rit)*.

حَلاوة *halva* is a dense, sweet, crumbly confection made with tahini and sugar, sometimes containing nuts or dried fruit.

اِوْعَى (f. اِوْعِي ; pl. اِوْعوا) + bare imperfect verb = *be careful not to*

—حاضِر.
—ميس منال عليْك النّهارْده؟
—ها.
—طيِّب شِدّ حيلك عشان تِدّيلك درجه كوُيِّسه مِش زَيّ المرّه اللى فاتِت لمّا زِعِلِت مِنّك.

مفيش حاجه ميدو بيْحِبّها اكْتر مِن البطاطِس المُحمّره فى الدُّنْيا. هُوَّ مُسْتعِدّ ياكُلْها فِطار و غدا و عشا. بدأ يِسْتمْتِع ميدو بِفْطارهُ لمّا سِمع صوْت باباه اللى طِلع مِن الحمّام بيْقولُّه: "يَلّا قوم عشان **تِلْحق** توْصل و خُد الخمْسه جْنيْه دى عشان ترْكب و تِشْتِريلك كيس شيبْسى وَلّا عصير مِن الكانْتين."

ميدو خد الفلوس مِن **باباه و مامْتُه** حطِّتْلُه السّنْدويتْشات فى جيب الشّنْطه و زَيّ كُلّ يوْم قالِت و هِيَّ بِتْساعْدُه يِلْبِس الشّنْطه: "**يا ساتِر!** الشّنْطه دى تِقيله كِده ليْه، ايْه بِتْحُطُّه فيها طوب مِش كُتُب؟"

لِبِس ميدو شنْطِتُه و خرج مِن البيْت و مامْتُه بِتْقولُّه الوَصايا المُعْتاده: "معَ السّلامه يا حبيبى. علىَ مهْلك و انْتَ بِتِنْزِل مِن الميكْروباص. لوْ حدّ غريب كلِّمك متْرُدِّش عليْه، فى امان الله."

"Yes, mom."

"Is Miss Manal teaching you today?"

"Yes."

"Okay, do your best so she gives you a good grade, unlike last time when she wasn't so happy with you."

There's nothing Mido likes more in the world than French fries. He would eat them for breakfast, lunch, and dinner. Mido was enjoying his breakfast when he heard his father coming out of the bathroom saying to him, "Get moving so you arrive on time, and take this five pounds to get the microbus and buy yourself a bag of chips or juice from the cafeteria."

Mido took the money from his dad while his mom put the sandwiches in his backpack, and just like every day while she's helping him put on his backpack, she said, "Dear God! This bag is so heavy! What do you put in it, rocks or books?"

Mido put on his backpack and left home while his mom said her usual commandments, "Goodbye, honey! Get off the microbus carefully. If a stranger talks to you, don't reply. God protect you!"

لِحِق (يِلْحَق) + bare imperfect verb = *have time to (do) or do in time (before it's too late)*

بابا retains the final ـا when a suffix is added: بابايا *my father,* باباه *his father,* باباها *her father.* However, the final ـا of ماما becomes ـتـ because it is feminine and treated like taa marbuta (ـة): ماْمتي *my mother,* ماْمتُه *his mother,* ماْمِتها *her mother.*

يا ساتِر is an expression of dismay. ساتِر (lit. *protector*) is an epithet of God.

قعدِت أمّ عمرو ترْتاح شُوَيّه إنّها خِلصِت من واحد فيهُم و تِشمّ نفسْها قبْل ما تْقوم تكمّل نفْس الفيلم معَ إخْواتُه. و جه الدّوْر علَى هِبه بِنْتها الكِبيره اللى فى جامْعِة القاهِره كُلّيّة الاداب قِسْم عِلْم نفْس.

"يا هِبه..يا هِبه.." بِتْهِزّها و تِشِدّ الغطا مِن عليْها. "انتِ يا بِتّ! يلّا عشان مُحاضْرتِك السّاعه ٩، السّاعه بقِت ٨ اهىْ."

قامِت هِبه مخْضوضه بِتْبُصّ فى الموبايْل بِنُصّ عيْن السّاعه بقِت كام، لقِت السّاعه لِسّه ٨ الّا تِلْت. قامت هِبه متْعصّبه مش مِصدّقه ازّاى مامِتها بِتِعْرف تِضحك عليْها كُلّ مرّه و تِبالغ و هِيّ بِتْقولْها السّاعه كام. و طبْعاً **زَيّها** فى كِده **زَيّ** كُلّ الأُمّهات المِصْريه الاصيله.

قرّرِت هِبه تِعْفى مامِتْها مِن مُعاناة تصْحيّة عمْرو اليوْم ده و تِقوم هِيَّ بِالدّوْر ده.

—يا عمْرو..مِش هتْقوم بقَى؟ قوم روح المدْرسه ولّا ذاكِر شُوَيّه عشان درْس التّاريخ..يا واد يا عمْرو!
—اِسْكتى شُوَيّه! سيبينى!
—قوم **يا ابْنى** بدل ما اخلّص كُلّ الطعْميه و البطاطِس و مِش هسيبْلك.
—يوووه! طيّب طيّب خلاص **قُمْت اهو**.

—صباح الخيرْ يا بابا. صباح الخيرْ يا ماما، هِبه قالِت لِباباها و مامِتْها.

Om Amr sat down to rest a little now that she had gotten rid of one of them and to catch her breath before the same scene would play out with his brother and sister. Now it was Heba's turn, her eldest daughter, who was at Cairo University, Faculty of Arts, department of psychology.

"Heba... Heba..." She shook her and pulled off the covers. "Hey, girl! Hurry to get to your lectures at nine. It's eight now!"

Heba jumped up, freaked out, and squinted at her cell phone to check the time, and saw it was still 7:40. Heba got up annoyed, not believing how her mom could pull that over on her every time, exaggerating the time. Just a typical Egyptian mom.

Heba decided to save her mom the fuss of waking Amr up that day and to do it herself.

"Amr, aren't you getting up? Go to school or study a bit for your history class. Amr!"

"Shut up! Leave me alone!"

"Get up or I'll eat all the falafel and French fries and not leave you any."

"Arghhh! Okay, okay! I'm up."

"Good morning, Dad! Good morning, Mom!" Heba said to her parents.

تِسْعه = ٩

تمانْيَه = ٨

اهو (m.) and اهيْ (f.) are particles that follow a phrase to emphasize or draw attention to it.

زَيّ... زَيّ = *just like*

يا ابْنى (lit. *my son*) – Notice that Heba says this to her brother mockingly. Such usage of forms of address is common among Egyptians.

محدِّش ردّ عليْها. ابوها كان مِركِّز فى اللَّاب توب بتاعُه و فى إيدُه كوبّاية الشّاى، و مامتها كانِت بدأت خلاص روتين كُلّ يوْم فى ترْويق البيْت مطْرح ما ميدو سايب بيجامْتُه و شراباتُه و حاجْتُه.

قعدِت هِبه تِفْطر و نادِت:
— ماماا..ماماا..فينْ كوبّاية الشّاى بلبن بتاعْتى؟
— حاضِر حاضِر..هصُبّهالِك اهو. خُفت اصُبّهالِك مِن بدْرى تِبرْد.
— شُكْراً يا ماما يا حبيبْتى.

باعْتِبار هِبه البِنْت الوَحيده فا هيَّ اللى حدّ ما دلّوعِة باباها و مامتْها وسْط الولديْن. بسّ مِش زَىّ ميدو اخِر العنْقود اللى مامْتُه بِتْخاف عليْه اكْتر مِنْهُم كُلُّهُم.

— عاوْزانى اعْمِلِّك حاجه تاخْديها معاكى الجامْعه؟
— ايه الكلام ده بسّ يا ماما! اِنْتى عاوْزه النَّاس تِضْحك عليَّا! لا طبْعاً هشْتِرى سنْدويتْش مِن الكافِتِرْيا.
— **طب يا سِتّى حقُّك عليَّا!**

اخيراً عمْرو **بيْه شرّف** و جه يِفْطر. قعد علَى الطَّربيْزه بدون كلام و هُوَّ مِكشِّر و بدأ ياكُل. فضِلت هِبه باصّالُه خايْفه تِتْكلِّم و هُوَّ مِقْريف كِده لانُّه بِيكْرهْ الصّحْيان بدْرى.

No one responded. Her father was focused looking at his laptop with a cup of tea in one hand, while her mom had already begun her daily routine of picking up the house wherever Mido left his pajamas, socks, and things.

Heba sat down to have breakfast and called, "Mom! Mom! Where's my cup of tea with milk?"

"All right, all right, I'm making it. I didn't want to pour it for you earlier or it'd get cold."

"Thanks, my lovely mom."

Heba, being the only girl among the children, was more or less spoiled by her parents, but not as much as Mido, the youngest child, whose mother worried about him the most.

"Do you want me to make you something to eat at the university?"

"What are you talking about, Mom? Do you want people to laugh at me? Of course not! I'll buy a sandwich from the cafeteria."

"All right, sorry I asked!"

At last Mr. Amr showed up to breakfast. He sat down at the table without saying a word. He was grumpy and started eating. Heba looked at him scared to talk when he was that fussy, as he really hates waking up early.

طب = طيِّب (interjection to express agreement or begin an utterance or response) *well, then, okay*

حقّك عليّا (sincere or sarcastic apology) *I'm sorry!; My bad!*

بيْه an overly formal and old-fashioned title nowadays commonly used to flatter, or, as here, to show sarcasm.

شرّف *to honor (with one's presence)* (here, used sarcastically)

بعْد صمْت طَويل ابو عمْرو قال: "ماشى يا ولاد انا هنْزِل انا عشان اَلْحق افْتح الصَّيْدليه. عاوْزين حاجه؟"

قبْل ما يخلّص الجُمْله ردّ عمْرو و هِبه فى نفْس الوَقْت:
— عاوْزين المصْروف!
— طبْعاً طبْعاً، مُسْتحيل تِنْسوا حاجه زَىّ كِده. اِتْفضّل يا سيدى. اِتْفضّلى يا ستّى.

— شُكْراً يا بابا.

وَدّعِت أُمّ عمْرو ابو عمْرو: "معَ السّلامه، اِبْقَى هات لِلولاد فاكهه و اِنْتَ جاىّ." و هزّ ابو عمْرو راسُه و قفل الباب.

— يَلّا يا بِنْت اِنْتى و هُوَّ عشان تِلْحقوا المدْرسه و المُحاضَرات.
— حاضِر يا ماما، الاِتْنيْن فى نفْس الوَقْت.
— تِحِبّ نِرْكب سَوا المِتْرو؟ قالِت هِبه لِعمْرو.
— لا شُكْراً، هروح معَ ناس صُحابى.
— ماشى.

وقِفِت هِبه قُدّام الدّولاب تِفكّر زَىّ كُلّ يوْم. "انا معنْديش حاجه اَلبِسْها." اخيراً اِسْتقرّت علَى شِميز و بنْطلون جينْز و لفّت **طرْحِتْها** و بدأ اكْتر جُزْء تحدّى فى اليوْم:

After a long silence, Abu Amr said, "Okay, kids, I'm taking off to open the pharmacy. Do you need anything?"

Before he even finished his sentence Amr and Heba both replied, "We want our pocket money!"

"Sure, sure. You can't ever forget something like that. Here you are, sir. Here you are, miss."

"Thank you, dad."

Om Amr walked Abu Amr to the door and said, "Goodbye, buy some fruit for the kids on your way home." Abu Amr nodded and closed the door behind him.

"Hurry, you two, so you don't miss school and your lectures."

"Okay, Mom," they said in unison.

"Do you want to take the subway together?" Heba asked Amr.

"No thanks. I'm going with my friends."

"Okay."

Heba stood in front of her wardrobe like every day. "I have nothing to wear." Finally, she settled on a blouse and jeans and tied her headscarf and then the most challenging part of her day began:

طرحة *headscarf* – Egyptian women typically do not wear headscarves at home. They will put them on shortly before leaving the house and take them off upon arriving home, as long as only relatives or other women are present. They will leave their headscarves on in the presence of company or male cousins. Of course, women must cover their heads to perform prayers, as well.

ظبْط الاى لاينْر! بعْد وَقْت مِن المسْح و التّظْبيط نِجْحِت هِبه فى مُهِمِّتها و بصِّت بصّه اخيره فى المرايَه و طِلْعِت. "يَلّا سلامْ يا مامْتى!" و جِرْيِت ناحْيةِ الباب قبْل ما مامِتْها تِلْحق تقول كالعاده: "ايْه البنْطلون الضّيّق ده؟ روحى غيّرى هِدومِك!"

عمْرو كمان طِلع مِن الاوْضه لابِس اوّل حاجه لقاها قُدّامُه مِن كوْمةِ الهِدوم اللى علَ الكُرْسى: بنْطلون اِسْود و تى شيرْت. و فتح الباب و نِزِل.

"عمْرو..؟"

طِلْعِت أُمّ عمْرو مِن المطْبخ بعْد ما خلّصِت غسيل مَواعين الفِطار تتْأكِّد اِنّ عمْرو اللى فتح باب الشّقّه و لقِت البيْت كُلُّه نِزِل خلاص و زَىّ كُلّ يوْم قالِت: "هعْمِل غدا ايه النّهارْده...؟"

Matching the eye-liner! After some time removing and adjusting, Heba completed her mission and took a final look in the mirror before she left. "Goodbye, mom!" And she ran to the door before her mom could say anything like "Those pants are too tight. Go change!"

Amr also left his room, wearing the first thing he saw in the pile of clothes on the chair: black pants and a t-shirt. He opened the door and left.

"Amr?"

Om Amr went out of the kitchen after she finished washing the dishes to check if it was Amr who had opened the door of the house. She found the house empty, and, as every day, she said, "What should I cook for lunch today?"

نِزِل (يِنْزِل) (lit. *to descend*) is used idiomatically to mean *to go out, leave the house*

الفصل التانى: المحطّه الخاطِئه

صوْت جرس الحِصّه الاخيره زَىّ المزّيكا فى ودْن ميدو و صُحابُه. اوِّل ما العِيال تِسْمعُه بِتِطلع تِجْرى زَىّ اللى سِمِع اِنْذار الحريقه. **هُجووووم علىَ** باب الفصْل و زقّ علىَ السّلالِم و اخيراً كُلّ المدْرسه بِتِتْحِشِر فى الباب الحديد اللى الخُروج منُّه هُوَّ غاية كُلّ العِيال اللى مِسْتنِّيين اللّحْظه دى مِن السّاعه ٧ الصُّبْح.

بعْد معْركِة الاِنْصِراف ميدو و كُلّ العِيال طالْعين فى حاله اَىّ اُمّ لَوْ شافِتْها هَيُغْمَى عليْها، قميص مِكرْمِش و طالع مِن البنْطلون، بُقع مجْهوله المصْدر مُخْتلِفه علىَ القميص، و طبْعاً كوتْشى رُباطُه مفْكوك.

مِشى ميدو بِخطْوات بطيئه مُرْهقه مِن اليوْم الطّويل فى المدْرسه.

النّهارْده مُدرِّس الرِّياضِيّات **مِسْتر** محْمود كان غايِب و خدوا حِصّة

Chapter 2: **The Wrong Station**

The last class's bell is like music to the ears of Mido and his friends. Once the students hear it, everyone runs as if it were the fire alarm. Everyone rushes to the classroom door, pushes down the stairs, and finally the whole school gets jammed at the iron gates of the school, getting through which is the goal of all the kids, who have been waiting for this moment since 7 a.m.

After the battle of leaving school, Mido and all the kids are in a such a state that if any mother saw, she would faint. A wrinkled, untucked shirt, various stains from unknown sources on the shirt, and, of course, loose shoelaces.

Mido walked slowly, exhausted from the long day at school.

Today, the math teacher, Mr. Mahmoud, was absent, so

هُجوم علّى (lit. *an attack on*) is used as a battle cry: *Chaaarge!*

سبْعه = ۷

مِسْتر and ميس are borrowed from the English *Mister* and *Miss,* respectively, and are the titles and forms of address for school teachers in Egypt.

اَلْعاب مكانْها، و ده طبعاً معْناه كوْره و زقّ و شدّ و رمْله. ميدو كمان جعان جِدًّا. فيه حدّ سرق سنْدويتْش الحلاوَه بِتاعُه لمّا ساب شنْطِتُه فى الفصل و نزِل حِصِّة الالْعاب.

وَصل ميدو اخر الشّارع و اِتْهِّد فى يأْس، لِسّه فيه معْركه كمان: لازِم ميدو يكْسبْها و هِيَّ ركُوب المِيكْروباص. كُلّ النّاس اللى واقْفه علىَ المحطّه بتِسْتنَّى ميكْروباص رمْسيس و اوِّل ما بيِيجى ميدو مِش بيْحِسّ بنفْسُه غير و هُوَّ بيرْكب بقُوَّة الدّفع. ميكْروباصات كتيره جت و هُوَّ لِسّه مِستنّى، لِحدّ ما جِه الفرج، أوْ اللحْظه الحاسمه! ميكْروباص رمْسيس!

جرى ميدو ناحْية الميكْروباص زَيّ النّاس الكتيره اللى جرْيت و حاوِل يِشُقّ طريقُه للباب لكِن شنْطتُه الحمْرا اِتْحشرت وَراه بين النّاس اللى بيِتْدافع. ميدو اللى صعب علىَ ستّ كِبيره شدِّتُه بِسُرْعه و قعّدتُه جُوَّ جنْب الشِّبّاك عشان محدِّش يِخْبطُه.

بدأ الميكْروباص يِتْحرِّك و **التبّاع** نادى "اللى مدفعْش الاُجْره يا حضرات!" و كالعاده بدأ تجْميع الاُجْره و جُمل زَىّ "واحِد مِن الخمْسه..اِتْنين مِن العشره..و اللى وَرا لِسّه راكِب و مدفعْش.." الىَ اخرِه..*

they had a P.E. class in that time slot. That means soccer, pushing, pulling and dust. And Mido was so hungry. Someone had stolen his halva sandwich when he left his backpack in class and went out for P.E.

Mido reached the end of street and sighed in despair; there is still one more battle Mido has to win: getting on the microbus. Everyone in the station was waiting for the Ramses microbus. As soon as it came, Mido found himself being pushed among the crowd. Lots of microbuses came but he was still waiting, until the wait was over! The decisive moment! The Ramses microbus!

Mido ran toward the microbus just like all the people running. He tried to find a way to the door but his red backpack got stuck among the crowd behind him. An old lady felt sorry for Mido and quickly pulled him in and gave him the seat next to the window so no one would bump him.

The microbus started moving, and the conductor called out, "Who hasn't paid yet, ladies and gentlemen?" And as usual, people started collecting the fares and saying sentences such as "One fare from five pounds!" "Two fares from ten!" "The man sitting in the back hasn't paid yet." etc..

وَصِل is also, and perhaps more commonly, pronounced وِصِل.

تبّاع *conductor,* for lack of a better translation. The تبّاع works on a bus or minibus, often hanging out of the open door, shouting the destination and looking for passengers, as well as collecting fares from passengers, and otherwise assisting the driver.

*Passengers typically help pass up fares to the front and pass back change.

ميدو طلّع الجنيْه الفضّه و إدّاه للسِّتّ اللى جنْبُه. و قال: "الطّريق اكيد هَيْكون واقِف جدّاً. **لمّا** اسْنِد راسى و اناملى شُوَيّه." غمض ميدو **عيْنُه** و راح فى نوْم عميق و مصحيش غير علىَ دَوْشه و ناس كِتيره بِتنْزِل مرّه واحده. اِتْفزع ميدو و قال بصوْت عالى: "رمْسيس رمْسيس! ثَوانى **يا اسْطىَ**!" و نِزِل بِسُرْعه جدّاً.

بصّ ميدو قُدّامُه و مِش شايف أىّ حاجه مِن المعالِم المُعْتاده اللى بيْشوفْها اوِّل ما بِينْزِل: معْصرة القصب، البيّاع بِتاع الجرايِد و اهمّ علامه محطّة مصْر! فيْن محطّة مصْر؟!

فكّر ميدو بخوْف: "يِمْكِن..يِمْكِن..يِمْكِن انا نِزِلْت قُدّام شُوَيّه فا لوْ مِشيت وَرا هلاقى رمْسيس." مِشى ميدو و مِشى و ملقاش رمْسيس بسّ لقىَ حاجه تانْيَه احْسن بِكْتير! لقىَ مكان مليان كُتُب و لِعب و اكْل و شُنط و تقْريباً كُلّ حاجه!

ميدو نِسى علىَ طول الخوْف و جِرى بِسعاده بيْن البيّاعين. وِقِف يِتْفرّج علىَ البيّاع اللى بيِسْتعْرض اللُّعب اللى بيْبيعْها، مِن اوِّل الكلْب اللى بيِتْشقْلِب و يِهَوْهَوْ و سبونْج بوب اللى بيِنْفُخ فُقعات صابون لِحدّ الرّوبوْت الصُّغيرّ اللى بيِضْرب ليزر. حطّ ميدو إيدُه فى جيْبُه يِشوف فِضِل معاه كام مِن مصْروفُه و لقىَ ٣ جنيْه معْدن. و سأل:

—عمّو..بِكام الرّوبوْت ده؟
—بِخمْسه جِنيْه.
—شُكْراً.

Mido got out a pound coin and gave it to the lady next to him. He said to himself, "The road must be really congested. I'll lean my head on the window and get myself a little sleep." Mido shut his eyes and went into a deep sleep and only woke up at the noise of lots of people getting off the microbus at once. Mido panicked and shouted, "Ramses! Ramses! Wait, driver!" and he got off quickly.

Mido looked in front of him and didn't see any familiar landmarks that he normally sees when he gets off: the cane juice press, newspaper vendor, and most importantly, Ramses station! Where is Ramses station?!

Scared, Mido thought, "Maybe, maybe, maybe I missed my stop, and if I go back, I will find Ramses." Mido walked and walked but didn't find Ramses. However, he found something else much better! He found a place full of books, toys, food, bags and almost everything!

Mido immediately forgot about his fear and ran happily between the vendors. He stopped to watch the vendor who was demonstrating the toys he sells. From a dog that flips and barks, and a Sponge Bob that blows bubbles, to a little robot with a flashing "laser". Mido put his hands in his pockets checking how much he has left from his pocket money, and he found three one-pound coins.

He asked, "Sir, how much is that robot?"

"Five pounds."

"Thank you."

لمّا (lit. *when*) here, does not mean *when* but is used idiomatically before a first-person bare imperfect verb to signify you're just about to do something. It might translte *I'll* or *Let me just...*

عيْن – Notice that the singular is often used in Egyptian Arabic for a pair of body parts, such as eyes, ears, hands, and legs.

يا اسْطَى is the common form of address to a bus or taxi driver.

تلاته = ٣

مِشى ميدو زعْلان انّ فِلوسُه مكفِتْش. بسّ شمّ ريحه جميله جدّاً فكّرتُه ادّ ايه هُوَّ كان جعان: عربيه بتْبيع سندويتْشات كِبده و سُجُقّ. صحيح مامْتُه قالتْلُه ممْنوع اكْل الشّارع، بسّ هُوَّ كان واقع مِن الجوع و تعْبان.

—**عمّو**..بكام السّنْدويتْش؟
—بجنيْه الصّغيَّر و باتْنيْن الكِبير.
—عاوِز واحِد صُغيَّر.

خد ميدو السّنْدويتْش و قعد علَى جنْب ياكْلُه. كان طعْمُه مُخْتلف عن الكِبده اللى مامْتُه بتِعْملها فى البيْت بسّ كانِت حِلْوَه و حرّاقه شُوَيّه. لمّا خلّص ميدو السّنْدويتْش حسّ بعطش شديد. شاف عربيه تانْيه و راجل بيْبيع عصير تمْر هِنْدى و عرق سوس. جرى ميدو و ادّالُه تانى جنيْه معاه و قالُه: "عاوِز تمْر هِنْدى مِن فضْلك."

التّمْر هِنْدى المتلّج سقَى عطش ميدو و بقَى دِلْوَقْتى مِصحْصح و مِش جعان. و بنشاط جِرى ناحْية اكْشاك الكُتُب اللى مِن كُلّ لوْن و لِكُلّ سِنّ. فِضِل يِتْمشَّى و يِتْفرّج علَى الكُتُب المُسْتعمله و الجديده، كُتُب عِلْميه و ادبيه و ترْفيهيه، لحدّ ما وصِل لِكنْز. حيْطه كامْله مِن مجلّات ميكى. تلال و تلال مِن الاعْداد. حاجات مِن قبْل ما يِتْوِلد هُوَّ موْجوده. عينيْه كانت بِتِلْمع، كان نفْسُه يُقْعُد وِسْط المجلّات دى كُلّها و يِنسُوه لِلابد.

البيّاع شافُه و قرّب مِنُّه و قالُه: "تِحِبّ انقّيلك عدد؟ ايْه رأيَك فى ده؟" و شدّ مجلّه عليْها ميكى راكِب سفينه و معاه بُنْدُق و الموْج عالى. المجلّه اه كان ورقْها دايب بسّ ميدو كان لِسّه عاوِزْها جدّاً.

Mido walked away, sad that his money wasn't enough. But he smelled a wonderful smell that reminded him how hungry he was: a cart that sells liver and sausage sandwiches. Although his mom told him no street food, he was starving and so tired.

"Sir, how much is a sandwich?"

"A small is one pound, and a large is two."

"I'll have a small one."

Mido took the sandwich and sat on a corner eating it. It tasted different than the liver his mom cooked at home, but it was delicious and a little spicy. When Mido finished the sandwich, he felt very thirsty. He saw another cart and vendor that sells tamarind juice and licorice juice. Mido ran and gave him the second pound he had and said, "I'd like a tamarind juice, please."

The icy cold tamarind juice quenched Mido's thirst, and now he was refreshed and full. He briskly ran towards the book stalls, with books of every color and for all ages. He kept walking and looking at the used and new books—scientific, literary, and entertaining books—until he came upon a treasure. An entire wall of Mickey Mouse magazines. Piles and piles of issues. There were even some from before he was even born. His eyes were glowing, and he wished he could sit between all these magazines and be forgotten forever.

The vendor saw him, came up to him, and asked him, "Would you like me to choose an issue for you? What about this one?" He pulled out a magazine with Mickey on the cover on a ship with Goofy and the waves were high. The pages of the magazine were worn out, but Mido still wanted it badly.

عمّو (lit. *uncle*) is a polite form of address by children to adult men. To women, children can say طنْط (borrowed from the French word *tante*).

ميدو بِسُرْعه حطّ اِيدُه فى جيْبُه و طلّع اخِر جِنيْه معاه و اِدّاه للرّاجِل و شدّ المجلّه مِنُّه و جِرى. راح قعد علىَ كُرْسى بِمِظلّه و بِإنْبِهار فتح وَرقات المجلّه و بدأ يِقْرا.

لمّا رفع عيْنُه ميدو لقَى الشّمْس بِتْغْرُب و السّما بقِت بُرْتُقانى. اِتْخضّ ميدو و قال: "البيْت! البيْت! لازِم **اروّح**! و افْتِكر اِزّاى اِدّى للرّاجِل بيّاع المجلّه اخِر جِنيْه معاه.

جِرى بِسُرْعه لِبيّاع المجلّات اللى بصّلُه و عيْنُه بِتِلْمع اِنُّه كِسِب زُبون لُقْطه:

—ايْه؟ خلّصتها و عاوِز واحْده تانْيه؟
—لا لا. انا اِدّيْتك اخِر جِنيْه معايا و لازِم ارْكب و اروّح البيْت، الوَقْت اِتْأخّر. مُمكِن مِن فضْلك تِدّينى الجِنيْه بِتاعى و تاخُد المجلّه؟
—اِنْتَ اِتْجنّنْت؟ عاوِز تِقْرا المجلّه و بعْديْن تِرْجعْها؟! اِنْتَ فاكِرْنى **مكْتبه**؟ انا محلّ! اِمْشى مِن هنا!

مِشى ميدو و هُوَّ خايِف و عينيْه مِدمّعه و مِش عارِف يعْمِل ايْه. شافُه راجِل و هُوَّ قاعِد علىَ جنْب بِيعيّط.

—مالك يا ابْنى؟

Mido put his hand in his pocket and took out the last pound he had and gave it to the man. He grabbed the magazine from him and ran off. He went and sat on a chair with a canopy and, fascinated, he opened the pages of the magazine and started to read.

When Mido looked up, he found the sun was setting and the sky was orange. Mido freaked out and said, "Home! Home! I must get home." He remembered how he had given the magazine vendor the last pound he had.

Mido quickly ran to the magazine vendor, who looked him with his eyes glowing that he had won over a great customer.

"What? You've finished it and want another one?"

"No, no. I gave you the last pound I had, and I have to take the microbus to get home, and it's late. Can you please give me my pound back and take the magazine?"

"Are you crazy? You want to read the magazine and then give it back?! Do you think I'm a library? I'm a vendor! Get out of here!"

Mido walked, scared, with tears in his eyes, not knowing what to do. A man saw him sitting on the curb crying.

"What is wrong, young man?"

روّح *to go home;* not to be confused with راح *to go*

لُقْطه *rare find, lucky find*

مكتبه can also mean *bookstore,* and is used in the names (on signs) of bookstores, but in common usage, it is understood as *library,* while محلّ كُتُب is used to mean *bookstore.*

معيش فِلوس اروّح البيْت و مِش عارِف انا فيْن.
—طيِّب عارِف رقم بيتْكو؟

رفع ميدو راسُه و عيْنُه وِسْعِت فى امل:
—اه..اه..ماما بِتْحفِّظونى علىَ طول!
—كُوَيِّس جِدّاً..تعالَ نِتِّصِل بيهُم ييجوا ياخْدوك.

خد الرّاجِل ميدو لِحدّ كُشْك عنْدُه تِليفوْن و شال ميدو عشان يِضْرب الرّقم و اِدّالُه السّمّاعه.

—الوْ؟ جه صوْت هِبه القلْقان مِن السّماعه.
—أَيْوَه يا هِبه. انا ميدو..
—ميدو! اِنْتَ فيْن كُلّ ده! اِحْنا هنِتْجنِّن عليْك! بابا نِزِل بِدوّر عليْك هُوَّ و عمر..!

مامِتْها جِرْيِت شدِّت السّمّاعه:
—ميدو! حبيبى! اِنْتَ فيْن؟
—انا كُنْت راكِب رمْسيس و نمْت و بعْديْن..

قاطْعِتُه: "أَيْوَه يَعْنى اِنْتَ فيْن دِلْوَقْتى!"

—انا فيْن..؟
—فى **العتّبه**.

"I have no money to get home, and I don't know where I am."

"Well, do you know your home phone number?"

Mido looked up, and his eyes widened with hope:

"Yes, yes! Mom makes me memorize it all the time."

"Great! Come with me to call them to come and get you."

The man took Mido to a booth that had a phone and lifted Mido up to dial the number and gave him the receiver.

"Hello?" Heba's worried voice came out of the receiver.

"Heba, it's Mido."

"Mido! Where have you been? We're so worried about you! Dad went to look for you with Am..!"

Her mom ran and grabbed the phone. "Mido! Honey! Where are you?"

"I took the Ramses microbus and I fell asleep, then..."

She interrupted him, "Okay, where are you now?"

"Where am I?"

"In Attaba."

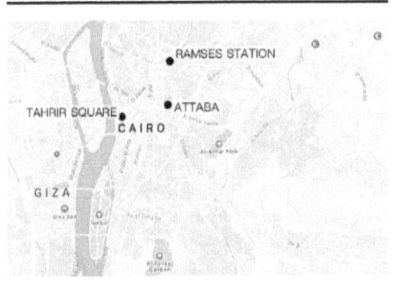

معيش is the more common, contracted form of ممعيش.

العتّبه *Attaba* is a district in central Cairo. (See map on left.)

—العتّبه.
—العتّبه!؟ قالِت مامْتُه. العتّبه كِبيره جِدّاً. فيه ايْه جنْبك؟
—انا فى مكان كُلُّه ناس بِتْبيع لِعب و ريموتات و هِدوم و كُتُب..كُتُب كِتير.

مامْتُه قالِت بِحماسه: "انا عِرِفْت انْتَ فينْ.. ميدو عنْد **سور الازْبِكيه**! بِسُرْعه يا هِبه كلِّمى بابا و عمْرو يِروحولُه هِناك."

—ماما..
—ايْوَه يا حبيبى؟
—مُمْكِن لمّا بابا يِيجى اشْتِرى الرّوبوْت اللى بِيِضْرب ليْزر؟ ده بِخمْسه جنيْه بسّ!

ضِحْكِت اُمّ عمْرو و قالِت: "الحمْدُ و الشُّكْر ليك يا ربّ."

"Attaba."

"Attaba!?" his mom said. "Attaba is so big. What's around you?"

"I'm in a place full of people selling toys, remote controls, clothes, books... a lot of books."

His mom said enthusiastically, "I know where you are. Mido's at Azbakeya Wall! Quickly, Heba, call your dad and Amr to go there."

"Mom..."

"Yes, honey?"

"When Dad comes, can he buy me the robot that flashes lasers? It's just five pounds!"

Om Amr laughed and said, "Thank God."

1 سور الازْبكيه *Azbakeya Wall* is home to a large second-hand book market with over a hundred book stalls and shops.

الفصْل التّالِت: **زِيارِة تيْته**

—**صباح الخيْر** يا ابو عمْرو. احضّرْلك الفِطار و كوبّايِة الشّاى؟
—صباح الخيْر، ردّ ابو عمْرو.

كمِّلِت أمّ عمْرو كلام: "بفكّر اخُد الوِلاد و اروح ازور ماما النّهارْده."

خرج ابو عمْرو مِن الحمّام و قعد عشان يِفْطر و كعادْتُه بِيْكون قُليِّل الكلام اوّل ما يِصْحَى.

قالِت أمّ عمْرو: "فيه اكْل مِن اِمْبارِح جاهِز تِسخّنُه و تِتْغدّى علَى طول اوّل ما تِخْلص فى الصّيْدليه."

رفع ابو عمْرو عيْنُه ليها و ردّ: "هتِرْجعوا السّاعه كام؟"

Chapter 3: **Visiting Grandma**

"Good morning, Abu Amr. Do you want me to make you breakfast and a cup of tea?"

"Good morning!" Abu Amr replied.

Om Amr continued, "I'm thinking of taking the children and go to visit my mom today."

Abu Amr came out of the bathroom and sat down to eat breakfast, and, as usual, when he's just woken up, he didn't talk much.

Om Amr said, "There is food from yesterday ready to be heated and eaten once you get back from work at the pharmacy."

Abu Amr looked up at her and asked, "When are you coming back?"

Good morning! and its responses:

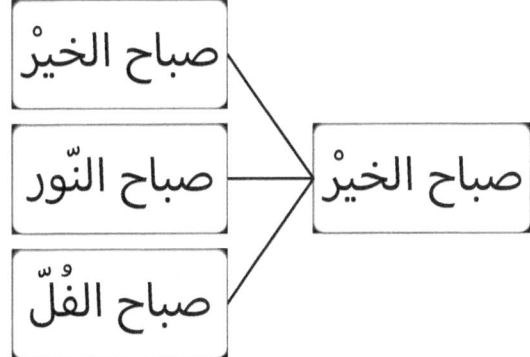

—يَعْنى علىَ المغْرِب وَلّا حاجه..تِحِبّ اجيبْلك حاجه و انا جايّه؟
—لا شُكْراً.

قام ابو عمْرو بعْد ما شِرِب كوبّايِة الشّاى و قرا الجُرْنان و بدأ يِلْبِس عشان يِروح يِفْتح الصَّيْدليه.
أمّ عمْرو قالِت: "خدْت كُلّ حاجه معاك؟ موبايْلك و المفاتيح؟ مِش ناسى حاجه؟"

هزّ ابو عمْرو راسُه فى هُدوء و خرج و قال و هُوَّ بيِفْتح باب الشّقّه: "سلامو عليْكو."

—و عليْكُم السّلام، فى امان الله.

فكّرِت أمّ عمْرو فى نفْسها: "خلِص الجُزْء السّهْل و بدأ الجُزْء الصّعْب." اِقْناع ابو عمْرو اِنّها تِسيبُه فى البيْت لِوَحْدُه و يِسخّن هُوَّ الغدا مِش زَىّ صُعوبِة تصْحيِّة العيال عشان يِروحوا لِجِدّتْهُم.

بدأِت مِن الاسْهل للاصْعب، مِن اوْضِة هِبه.

—هِبه..هِبه..اِصْحى عشان نِروح عنْد تيْته يلّا.
—مممم..هِبه بِتِتْقلِّب و تِغطّى وِشّها.
—يلّا يا هِبه عشان السّاعه ١٠ و بابا قال نِرْجع عَ المغْرِب.
—لا، روحوا اِنْتو. انا هخْرُج مَع صُحابى.

"Around sunset. Do you want me to get you something while I'm out?"

"No, thanks."

After Abu Amr had drunk the cup of tea and read the newspaper, he got up and went to get dressed to go and open the pharmacy.

Om Amr asked, "Have you got everything you need? Your cell phone and keys? Have you forgotten anything?"

Abu Amr shook his head slowly and went out saying, while opening the front door, "Goodbye!"

"Goodbye! May God protect you."

Om Amr thought to herself, "The easy part is over and now the difficult one starts." Convincing Abu Amr to stay alone at home and to heat the lunch by himself is not as difficult as waking the kids up to visit their grandmother.

She went from the easiest to the most difficult, starting with Heba's room.

"Heba... Heba... Wake up. We're going to visit Grandma."

"Hmm..." Heba turned over and covered her face.

"Come on! It's 10 o'clock and your dad said we should be home by sunset."

"You guys go. I'm going to go out with my friends."

سلامو عليكو is a more colloquial pronunciation of the Classical Arabic السّلامُ عليْكُم.

تيْته = جدّه grandmother

عشره = ١٠

عَ is a shortened form of علَى used before the definite article.

—تُخْرُجى ايه و زِفْت ايه! اِنْتى مشُفْتيش جِدِّتك بقالك ادّ ايه! لَوْ مِش هتيجى معانا هتُقْعُدى تِنضّفى الشّقّه و تِغْسِلى المَواعين و تِسخّنى الاكل لِابوكى لمّا ييجى! سامْعه؟

—يووّوْه..طيِّب خلاص! هاجى!

—يَلّا قومى و ساعْدينى اصحّى العِيال اِخْواتِك دول! قالِت أُمّ عمْرو و صوتْها بيِبْعد رايْحه لِاوْضِة الوِلاد.

—ميدو..عمْرو..يا وِلاد..يَلّا اصحوا رايْحين لِتيْته!

اوّل ما ميدو بيِسْمع رايْحين لِتيْته بيِفْرح جِدّاً. ميدو بيِحِبّ يزور جِدّتُه و كمان بيِحِبّ يرْكب **مِترْو المرْج** اللى بيِطْلع فوْق الارْض بيْن **قُصور القُبّه**.

قام ميدو بِسُرْعه و راح الحمّام غسل وِشُّه و طِلع عشان يِفْطر.

"صِحيت يا ميدو؟ شاطِر يا حبيبى... يا عمْرو!! اِنْتَ يا واد يا عمْرو!!" نادِت أُمّ عمْرو.

طِلعْت هِبه مِن اوضِتْها و قعدِت جنْب ميدو يِفْطروا و قالِت:

—ريّحى نفْسك يا ماما. عمْرو مِش هَيِصْحى بدْرى كِده وَلا هُوَّ بيْحِبّ يِروح عِنْد تيْته. هتْلاقى نازِل يِقابِل صُحابُه علىَ القهْوه.

"What 'going out' are you talking about?! How long has it been since you visited your grandmother? If you aren't coming with us, then you'll stay and clean the house, wash the dishes, and heat the food for you dad when he comes back! Do you hear me?"

"Ugh! Okay, okay! I'll come!"

"Get up and help me wake your brothers up!" said Om Amr while her voice came from the distance as she moved to the boys' room.

"Mido... Amr... Boys... Wake up! We're going to visit Grandma!"

As soon as Mido hears they are going to visit grandma, he feels so happy. Mido loves visiting his grandma and taking the El-Marg subway line, which comes up from the underground tunnels between the El-Qobbah palaces.

Mido got up quickly and went to the bathroom to wash his face and then went to eat breakfast.

"Have you woken up, Mido? Good boy... Amr... Amr!!" called Om Amr.

Heba came out of her room and sat next to Mido to eat breakfast.

"Save your breath, Mom." Amr won't wake up this early, and he doesn't like to go to Grandma's. He'll probably go and meet his friends at the coffee house."

مِترْو المرْج *the El-Marg subway line,* officially known as الخطّ الاوّل *Line One,* is the oldest and longest subway line in Cairo, with 35 stations along 27 miles (44 kilometers) of track.

قُصور القُبّه are two historic palaces in the القُبّه district of Cairo. They were once the residences of King Farouk.

—يَعْنى ايْه اِن شاء الله! لا طبْعاً، لازِم يِيجى معانا يِزور جِدُّتهْ.
أمّال محْسوب علينْا راجِل اِزّاى و عاوِز يِسيبْنا نِروح لِوحَْدِنا فى المُواصَلات؟

كمِّلت مُناداه: "انتَْ يا زِفْت!! لَوْ قُمْتِلك هرِنّك علْقه."

خرج عمْرو مِن اوضْتهُ مِتأفِّف و قال: "انا بتِْخنِق هناك! مبلاقيش حاجه اعْملْها و تِلفِْزيْوْن تيْته قديم و مفيش أىّ قنوات افلام كُويِّسه ولّا ماتْشات!"

—روح اقُْعُد معَ سِتّكَ شُوَيّه. كُلّ شُوَيّه تسِْأل عليَْك و تقِول عمْرو مِش بيِيجى يِزورْنى ليْه.
—يَعْنى انا و هىَّ هنْقول ايْه لِبعْض؟ بتِفِْضل تِقول أمُّك بتِشِْتِكى منّك..ذاكِر يا حبيبى عشان مُسْتقْبلكَ.
—يَعْنى الحقّ عليْها اِنّها قلْبها علىَ مصلْحْتك و عايزْه تِشوفكَ احْسن حدّ فى الدُّنْيا؟!
—طيِّب خلاص! هنْروح!

لبِسْوا كُلُّهمْ و جهّزِت أمُّ عمْرو شنْطه فيها بيِجامه لِميدو و جلّابيه ليها عشان تِساعِد مامِتْها فى توَْضيب الغدا. اِتأّكّدِت أمُّ عمْرو مِن اِنّها قفلت محابِس الميّه و انوْار الشّقّه و قفلِت الباب بِالمِفْتاح.

"What's that supposed to mean? Of course, he won't! He must come with us and see his grandmother. How is he considered a man if he'd let us go by ourselves on public transportation?"

She kept calling, "Hey, lazy! If I have to get you up, I'll give you a thrashing."

Amr came out of his room grumpy and said, "I get bored there! There's nothing to do and Grandma's TV is very old and there are no good movie channels or soccer matches!"

"Go spend some time with your grandma. She asks after you a lot and asks, 'Why doesn't Amr visit?'"

"What am I going to talk about with her? She always says 'your mom complains about you. Study, honey, for your future.'"

"Is she wrong that she wants what's best for you and that she wants you to be the best man in the world?"

"Okay, okay! I'll go."

They all got dressed, and Om Amr packed a bag with pajamas for Mido and a galabiya for herself to help her mom with making lunch. Om Amr made sure she turned off the water faucets and the apartment's lights and locked the front door with the key.

أُمّال is a particle that introduces a rhetorical or sarcastic question.

سِتّ normally means *woman,* but here, with a personal pronoun, it is a respectful synonym for جِدّه *grandmother.* (Note that it does not mean *grandmother* in the expression يا سِتّي *my dear lady.*)

جلّبيه *galabiya* is a traditionally Egyptian garment worn by both men and women. People will often wear them at home, feeling they are more comfortable than street attire. (See photograph on p. 79 of a man wearing a galabiya.)

حماسِة ميدو و هُوَّ بِيِنْزِل سلالِم المترو الكهربا و بِيْحاوِل يِمْشى بِسُرْعِه عشان يِكون جنْب عمْرو بتْخلّى مامْتُه تِتْضايِق و تُقْرُص عَلَى اِيدُه جامِد! "بسّ شقاوَه يا زفْت! هتوه فى الزّحمه اَوْ باب المترْو هَيِقْفِل عليْك!"

وِقْفوا مِسْتَنِّيين المِتْرو و رِكِبوا سَوا و جِرْيوا عَلَى اوِّل مكان فاضى شافوه. محطّه وَرا محطّه و ميدو مِسْتنّى المتْرو يِطْلع فوْق الارْض. اوِّل ما بدأتِ الشَّمْس تِظْهر فِرِح ميدو و بدأ بِيْبُصّ مِن الشَّبّاك علَى البِيوت و القُصور فى منْطِقة القُبّه و اخيراً بدأت منْطِقة جِدِّتُه تِظْهر و مامْتُه قالِت: "يَلّا يا ميدو، اِمْسِك اِيدى كُوَيِّس عشان محدِّش يِزُقّك و الباب مَيِقْفِلْش عليْك و اِنْتَ لِسّه جوّه."

ميدو دايْماً بِيْخاف يِحْصل زَىّ ما مامْتُه بِتْحذّرُه و يِلاقى نفْسه لِوَحْدُه جوّه المِتْرو و يِروح مكان مَيِعْرفوش. مِسِك فى اِيد مامْتُه بِخوْف و اوِّل ما سِمع موسيقِة فتْح الباب، نِزِل معاها بِسُرْعه و خد نفْسُه اِنّ الكابوس عدَّى.

رنّت أُمّ عمْرو الجرس اكْتر مِن مرّه لِحدّ ما مامِتْها فتحت الباب لِيهُم بِسبب سمعْها اللى ضعيف و خطَواتْها البطيئه. "اهْلًا و سهْلًا يا حبايِبى! اِتْفضّلوا اِتْفضّلوا."

Mido's enthusiasm while going down the subway escalators and his trying to walk fast to be next to Amr made his mom angry, so she held his hand tight. "Stop that, boy, or you'll get lost in the crowd or the subway doors will close on you."

They stood waiting for the subway, got in together, and ran toward the first empty seats they saw. Station after station, Mido is waiting for the subway to come out above ground. When sunlight started to appear, Mido was happy and looked from the window at the house and palaces in the neighborhood of El-Qobbah. And finally his grandmother's neighborhood appeared, and his mom said, "Come on, Mido. Hold my hand nice and good so no one pushes you and the door closes and you're still inside [the train]."

Mido is always afraid that what his mom warns him about will happen and he'll find himself alone on the subway going somewhere he doesn't know. He held his mother's hand in fear and as soon as he heard music before the doors open, he got off the train with her quickly and took a breath that the nightmare had passed.

Om Amr rang the doorbell more than once until her mom opened the door as she was hard of hearing and because of her slow steps. "Welcome, my darlings! Come in, come in!"

an above-ground Cairo subway station

بسّ here means *enough, stop, knock it off.*

شقاوه = naughtiness.

جِرى ميدو بِسَعاده لِجِدِّتُه اللى حِضنِتُه و باسِتُه و بدأت تِقولُه هِىَّ عامْلالُه ايْه النّهارْده مِن اكلها الجميل.

قعدوا كُلُّهُم فى الصّالونْ و بدأت تيتِتْهُم تِسْألْهُم علَى اخْبارْهُم كالعاده:
—**عامْله ايْه** يا هِبه فى الكُلّيه؟
—تمام يا تيْته.
—يَلّا **عُقْبال** ما نِفْرح بيكى و نِشوفِك عروسه.
—ان شاء الله.
—و انْتَ يا عمْرو، لِسّه تاعِب ماما و مِش بِتْذاكِر؟
—يَعْنى..بحا..

قاطعْتُه أُمّ عمْرو: "اه! تاعِبْنى فى الصّحَيان و فى المُذاكْره و علَى طول قاعِد قُدّام **الزِّفْت** اللّاب توْب!"

بصِّلها عمْرو فى ضيق و بِعِنْد طلّع موبايْلُه و بدأ شات معَ صُحابُه.

قالِت أُمّ عمْرو فى ضيق: "شُفْتى يا ماما! اهو فتح الموبايْل وَلا كان حدّ كِبير بِيِتْكلِّم معاه."
—**معْلِشّ** يا سامْيه (اِسْم أُمّ عمْرو الحقيقى) العِيال كُلّها مسيرْها تِكْبر و تعْقِل. ابو عمْرو عامِل ايْه؟
—اهو الحمْدُ لله ماشى الحال. طول اليوْم قاعِد فى الصّيْدليه.

Mido ran happily to his grandmother who hugged and kissed him and started telling him what she cooked him today of her delicious food.

They all sat in the living room and their grandmother started asking them about their lives, as usual.

"How is university, Heba?"

"Good, Grandma."

"Good. Hopefully, we will celebrate you being a bride soon."

"God willing."

"And you, Amr? Still giving your mom a hard time and not studying?"

"Well, I'm tr…"

Om Amr interrupted, "Yes! He's giving me a hard time getting him up and studying. He's always on his stupid laptop!"

Amr looked at her angrily, and in defiance, he pulled his cell phone out of his pocket and started chatting with his friends.

Om Amr said angrily, "See, Mom? He's on his phone now as if we're not talking to him."

"It's okay, Samya." (Om Amr's real name) "All kids will grow up and understand in their own time. How is Abu Amr?"

"He's fine. At the pharmacy all day."

عامِل ايْه؟ (f. عامْله ايْه؟; pl. عامْلين ايْه؟) literally means *What are you doing?* but is understood to mean *How is it going?* The response can be كْوَيِّس, تمام, etc.

عُقْبال commonly appears in wishes.

الزِّفْت + definite noun = *the stupid/damn/bloody* ___

معْلِش *It's okay!; No worries!; Don't worry about it!; Never mind!*

—ربّنا يِقوّيه... ها يا ميدو يا حبيبى! تعالَ احْكى لتِيْته المدرسه عامْله ايه! شطور وَلّا تاعِب ماما اِنْتَ كمان؟
—لا، ميدو شاطِر الحمْدُ لله! قالِت أمّ عمْرو.

قامت جِدِّتْهُم بخطَوات بطيئه و جابِت لميدو بُلوفر تِريكو عمِلتْهولُه و قالِتْلُه: "خُد يا حبيبى! عمِلْتِلك ده عشان يِدفّيك فى الشِّتا، و لوْنُه ازْرق اهو عشان يِناسِب لِبْس المدْرسه!"

فِرِح ميدو و جِرى باس سِتُّه.

—ليه بسّ تِعِبْتى نفْسِك يا ماما و اِنْتى نظركِ دِلْوَقْتى مِش لازِم تِتْعِبيه فى شُغْل التِّريكو.
—لا تعب وَلا حاجه! ميدو ده حبيبى.

لِبِسِت أمّ عمْرو الجلّابِيه و دخلِت المطْبخ هِيّ و الجِدّه يجهِّزوا الغدا و بدأِت الرّوايِح الحِلْوه تِمْلا الشّقّه. بعْد فتْره فرشوا الطّربيْزه و اِتْملِّت الطربيْزه محْشى و فِراخ و شورْبه و سلطه.

كُلُّهُم سابوا اللى فى اِيدْهُم. عمْرو ساب الموبايْل. هِبه قفلِت الفيلْم القديم. و ميدو ساب المجلّات اللى كان بِيِتْفرّج عليْها. و قعدوا فى حماسه عشان ياكْلوا عمايِل تِيْته.

"May God give him strength…. And you, Mido, my darling! Come tell your grandma about school! Are you clever or are you, too, giving your mom a hard time?"

"No, Mido's a good boy, thank God!" said Om Amr. Their grandmother got up slowly and brought Mido a knit sweater she had made for him and said, "Here, honey! I made this for you to keep you warm in the winter. It's blue to match your school uniform!"

Mido was happy and ran to kiss his grandmother.

"You shouldn't have gone to so much trouble, Mom. And you shouldn't be tiring your eyesight now with knitting."

"No trouble at all! Mido's my sweetie."

Om Amr put on the galabiya and went into the kitchen with their grandmother to start preparing lunch. Wonderful smells started to fill the apartment. After a bit, they set the table and it was covered with stuffed vegetables, chicken, soup, and salad.

Everyone put down what they were doing. Amr put down his phone, Heba turned off the old movie, and Mido put down the magazines he was looking at. They all sat down, excited to eat Grandma's cooking.

- يَلّا يا حبايْبي قولوا بِسْم الله و كُلوا. خيْر ربِّنا الحمْدُ لله كِتير.
- تِسْلم إيدِك يا تيْته! كُلُّهُمْ فى نفس واحِد.

بعْد ما كُلُّهُمْ شِبْعوا تيْته مرِضِتْش حدّ يقوم غيْر لمّا يِخلّص الطّبق قُدّامُه.

- مِش قادْرين يا تيْته والله.
- كِده؟ عاوْزينّى ازْعل مِنْكو؟
- والله ما قادْرين!
- شوفى ولادِك يا سامْيه!
- كُلّوا يا ولاد متْزعّلوش تيْته.

خلّصوا اكْل و قاموا. محدِّش قادِر يِتْنفّس بعْد الاكْل ده كُلُّه. قعدوا و كابِس عليْهُمْ النّوْم.

دخلِت أُمّ عمْرو تِغْسِل المَواعين و طِلْعِت لِبِسِت هِدومْها و نادِت: "يَلّا يا ولاد عشان يا دوب نِلْحق نِروّح البيْت قبْل المغْرِب."

"يا ولاد....!" دخلِت أُمّ عمْرو الصّالوْن لقِتْهُمْ كُلُّهُمْ ناموا بعْد الاكْله دي..

"Come on, kids. Say bismillah and start eating. God's blessings are many."

"Thank you, Grandma," they said in unison.

After they were full, their grandmother wouldn't excuse anyone until they had finished the plate in front of them.

"We can't eat more, Grandma. We swear."

"Is that so? You want to make me sad?"

"Honestly, we can't!"

"Say something to your kids, Samya!"

"Eat up, kids. Don't upset Grandma."

They finished eating and got up, unable to breathe after all that eating. They sat down, feeling sleepy.

Om Amr went to wash the dishes, then changed her clothes and called "Come on, kids! We need to get moving to make it home before sunset."

"Kids!!"

Om Amr went into the living room and found all of them asleep after all that food.

قال بِسْمِ الله *say bismillah,* or *basmala,* refers to the first verse in the Quran بِسْمِ اللهِ الرَّحْمٰنِ الرَّحِيْمِ (*In the name of God, the most gracious, the most merciful*), which Muslims utter before beginning any task, especially before eating a meal.

تِسْلَم إيدك (lit. *may your hands be safe*) is a formulaic expression to thank someone who has prepared a meal.

الفصْل الرّابِع: المعاد السِّرّي

يوْم الجُمْعه. صحْيِت هِبه لِوَحْدها مِن النّوْم بِكُلّ نشاط و بِابْتِسامه واسْعه. غسلِت وِشّها و خرجِت عشان تِفْطر. و كالعاده لقِت مامِتْها عامْله فِطار الجُمْعه الأُسْطورى: فول و طعْميه، بطاطس و جِبْنه بِطماطِم و بِتِنْجان مِخلِّل.

اوِّل ما أُمّ عمْرو شافِتْها: "خيْر خيْر صاحْيَه بدْرى يَعْنى و مِش زَىّ كُلّ مرّه تِتْعِبينا فى الصِّحْيان."

هِبه بِتوَتّر.."احمْم..لا انا بصْحَى عادى يا ماما..صباح الخيْر."
—طب روحى نادى علَى اِخْواتِك الصُّبْيان **عُقْبال ما** ابوكى يِطْلع مِن الحمّام.

"يا عمْرو..يا ميدو يَلّا الفِطار جاهِز و عشان تِلْحقوا تِروحوا تِصلّوا الجُمْعه..اِصْحوا يا وِلاد."

Chapter 4: **A Secret Rendezvous**

Friday. Heba woke up on her own feeling fresh and smiling. She washed her face and went to eat breakfast. As usual, she found her mom making the legendary Friday breakfast: beans, falafel, French fries, cheese with tomatoes, and pickled eggplant.

When Om Amr saw her, she said, "Well, well! You woke up on your own today, unlike most days when you give us a hard time waking you up."

Heba tensed up, "Ahem... No, I woke up, nothing special, Mom. Good morning!"

"Okay. Go and wake your brothers up before your dad comes out of the bathroom."

"Amr! Mido! Come on, breakfast is ready. [Get up] to get to the Friday prayer in time. Wake up, boys!"

عُقْبال ما = *by the time* (Note that it was used with the meaning *hopefully* on p. 42.)

الجُمْعه *Friday prayer* – Muslim men in Egypt generally go to their local mosque to listen to the weekly sermon and pray. With a large number of attendees, people may pray on the street outside the mosque, as well. Women mostly stay at home to pray, but if they do go to the mosque, they pray in a special area for women inside.

ميدو بسّ اللى قام مِن النّوْم و راح يِفْطر امّا عمْرو فِضِل نايِم و كالعاده بيِلْحق الصّلاه علَى الاخِر.

—صباح الخيْر يا ولاد، قال ابو عمْرو.
—صباح الخيْر يا بابا، ردّ ميدو و هِبه.

قعدوا كُلّهُم يِفْطروا و هِبه سرْحانه فى اللى هَيحْصل النّهارْده بعْد صلاة الجُمْعه.

—هِبه! يا بِتّ! سرحْتى فيْن؟
—ااه..**معاكى** يا ماما.
—هتِشْربى شاى بِلبن؟
—لا لا لا، شُكْراً.

مفيش وَقْت تِضيّعُه. المفْروض انّها يا دوْب تاخُد شاوَر و تِشوف هتِلْبِس ايه و تِحُطّ ميكب و تِنْزِل تِسْتنَّى احْمد عنْد محطّة ميتْرو الدُّقّى.

احْمد هُوَّ الوَلد اللى هِبه كانِت مُعْجبه بيه مِن زمان مِن الجامْعه. علَى طول بيُقْعُد معاها و مَع زمايلْها و يِتْكلّموا عادى بسّ دى اوَّل مرّه يِقولّها تِخْرُج معاه هيَّ لِوَحْدُهُم بعيد عن صاحْباتْها. يا ترَى هَيْقولّها ايه؟

فِضِلت هِبه تِتْخيّل حِوارات احْمد هَيْقولْهالْها زَىّ انّه مُعْجب بيها من اوّل ما شافْها، أوْ انّه كمان بيْحِبّها، أوْ انّه حتَّى عاوِز يِتْجوّزها!

Only Mido woke up and went to eat breakfast, but Amr kept sleeping, and as usual he'd barely make it for the last part of the prayer.

"Good morning, kids!" said Abu Amr.

"Good morning, Dad!" said Mido and Heba.

They sat down to eat breakfast. But Heba's mind was distracted by what would happen after the Friday prayer.

"Heba! Hey, you! What are you daydreaming about?"

"Huh? Nothing, Mom."

"Do you want a cup of tea with milk?"

"No. No, thanks."

There is no time to waste. She barely has time to take a shower, pick out something to wear, put on makeup, and then go to meet Ahmed at Dokki station.

Ahmed is the boy from college Heba has had a crush on for so long. He sits with her and her friends all the time, and they talk. But this is the first time he's asked her out alone away from her friends. She wondered what he would say to her.

Heba kept imagining conversations she'd have with Ahmed. That he would tell her that he's liked her from the moment he saw her. Or even that he loves her. Or... that he wants to marry her!

معاك literally means *with you,* as in *I'm (mentally) here, present with you.* It is the common response when you suddenly realize someone is trying to get your attention while you were daydreaming or absorbed in an activity.

فوّقِت هبه نفْسها مِن الاحْلام الوَرْدِيه و قالت: "بسّ بسّ بِشْويْش اوّل مرّه تِخرُجوا سَوا و داخله علَى جَواز يا هبْلَى يا مدْلوقه! لازِم تِبيّنى انّك تِقيله عليْه لحْسن يِطفِش."

دخلِت هبه خدِت شاوَر و طِلْعِت تِبُصّ للدّولاب. طلّعِت كُلّ حاجه تقْريباً و تِلْبِس و تِرْجع تِقْلع. تِلْبِس و تِقْلع. مفيش طقْم حاسّه انُّه حِلْو. احْمد معاها فى الجامْعه و بِيْشوفْها كُلّ يوْم و نِفْسها تِلْبِس طقْم جِديد فيه تغْيير.

فكّرِت هِبه فى حُزْن لوْ كان عنْدها اُخْت بِنْت كانِت اسْتلفِت مِنْها لِبْس أَوْ حتّى خدِت رأيْها لكِنّها وَحِيده وسْط اِتْنيْن صُبْيان و مامِتْها هتْزعّقْلها لوْ عِرفِت انّها هتُخْرُج مع وَلد.

قعدِت علَى السّرير فى اِسْتِسْلام و بعْديْن مرّه واحْده قامِت و جِرْيِت علَى الدّولاب و اِفْتكرِت طقْم كان عِنْدها ملِبْسِتوش غيْر مرّتيْن تلاته و زَىّ اَىّ بِنْت مصْريه ظبطِت معاه طرْحه و شنْطه بِلوْن مُخْتلِف و بِسعاده راحِت تِكْوِيه.

—اِنْتى رايْحه فيْن يا هِبه؟
—هخْرُج معَ صُحابى يا ماما. كُنْت قايْلالِك مِن يوميْن كِده.
—اه..هتْروحوا فيْن؟
—هنْروح وسْط البلد.
—معَ مِنّه و مَى؟

Heba pulled herself back to reality and thought to herself, "Whoa! Whoa! Slow down! It's your first date and you are dreaming of a proposal, you idiot! You've got to act cool or he'll run away."

Heba went to take a shower, got out, and looked in her wardrobe. She took practically everything out and started putting them on and taking them off, on and off. There wasn't a single outfit she felt looked nice. Ahmed is with her in college and sees her every day. She wanted to wear a new outfit for a change.

Heba thought sadly if only she had had a sister, she would have borrowed clothes from her or at least asked for her opinion, but she is alone with two brothers, and her mom would shout at her if she knew she was going on a date.

She sat on the bed in desperation. Then suddenly she got up and ran to the wardrobe, remembering a dress she had that she hadn't worn but two or three times. And like any Egyptian girl, she matched it with a contrasting headscarf and bag. Then she went happily to iron them.

"Where are you going, Heba?"

"I'm going out with my friends. I told you a couple days ago."

"Right. Where are you going?"

"Downtown."

"With Mennah and Mai?"

—ااا..اه معاهُم.
—ماشى سلِّمى عليْهُم و خلّوا بالكو مِن نفْسُكو و متِرْدُّوش علَى اَىّ شباب بيْعاكِس.
—حاضِر.

جِرْيِت هِبه و دخلِت اوضِتْها و مِسْكِت الموبايْل و بعتِت علَى جْروب صُحابْها البنات:
—بنات..ماما لَوْ اتِّصلِت علَى حدّ فيكو اِحْنا سَوا، ماشى؟!
—ماشى بسّ هُوَّ فيه ايْه؟ مِنّه ردِّت.
—مفيش مفيش هقولُكو بعْدَيْن، هِبه كتبِت.

زَىّ كُلّ المِصْريِّين محدِّش بيْحِبّ يِحْكى علَى حاجه لِحدّ ما تِمِرّ بِسلام الاوّل.

سِمْعِت هِبه مِن البلْكوْنه ادان الضُّهْر. "يالهْوى! الادان..مفيش وَقْت! هتْأخّر عليْه!"

بِسُرْعه بدأِت هِبه تِلْبِس و تحُطّ المناكير و تُنْفُخ فيه خايْفه يِلوَّس هِدومْها، و اخيراً بدأِت تحُطّ المِيكب. تحُطّ و تِمْسح، خفيف اوى، لا تِقيل اوى، لا مِش هَينْفع لِلنّهار، لا لوْنُه مِش لايِق.

"Uh... Yeah, with them."

"Okay. Tell them I say hello, and take care of yourselves, and don't talk to men who hassle you."

"All right."

Heba ran into her room, grabbed her cell phone and texted to the group chat with her girlfriends, "Girls, if mom calls, we are together, okay!?"

"Okay, but what's going on?" Menna replied.

"Nothing. I'll tell you later," Heba texted.

As with all Egyptians, no one likes to tell about anything until it successfully happens.

Heba heard from the balcony the call to the noon prayer. "Oh gosh! The call to prayer! There's no time. I'm going to be late!"

Quickly Heba started getting dressed, and put on nail polish, blowing at it so it wouldn't get on her dress. And finally, she started putting on makeup. Putting some on then removing it. *Too light. Too heavy. No, not suitable for daytime. No, the color doesn't match.*

بعْد مُحاوْلات طَويله هِبه بقِت جاهْزه و لِسَّه بِتْنهِّد بِسعاده و هِيَّ شايْفه نفْسها فى المرايَه. سِمْعِت "السَّلام عليكُم و رحْمِة الله، السَّلام عليكُم و رحْمِة الله.."

"الصَّلاه خِلْصِت؟! لازِم اجْرى!"

—ماما..
—نعم؟
—كُنْت..عاوْزه ٥٠ جنيْه.
—ليْه تانى؟ مِش معاكى مصْروف؟
—عشان..عشان هنِرْكب تاكْسى و هنُقْعُد فى كافيْه كُوَيِّس.
—اِتْفضَّلى يا أُسْتاذه.
—شُكْراً يا ماما.
—هِبه اِنْتى مِش حاطَّه مكْياج تقى..
—سلام يا ماما يا حبيبْتى! قاطْعِتْها قبْل ما تِكمَّل.

جِرْيِت هِبه و وَقَّفِت تاكْسى عشان ياخُدْها محطِّة الدُّقِّى، مكان ما هتْقابِل احْمد. قبْل ما توْصل لقيْته بيِتَّصِل. ردِّت بِتَوَتُّر: "الو..أيْوَه يا احمد، انا خلاص قرِّبْت..اِنْتَ عنْد المِترْو خلاص؟ ماشى انا جايَّه، سلام."

نزْلِت هِبه و شافِت احْمد قُدَّامها، اِبْتسِمْلها و قالِّها: "اِزيِّك؟"

After many attempts, Heba was ready at last. Looking at herself in the mirror, she was about to let out a sigh of satisfaction when she heard "As-salamu alaykum wa rahmatu Allah. As-salamu alaykum wa rahmatu Allah."

"The prayer's over?! I've got to run!"

"Mom!"

"Yes?"

"I... need 50 pounds."

"Why? Don't you have any pocket money?"

"It's to... to take a taxi and go to a nice café."

"Here you go, missy!"

"Thanks, Mom."

"Heba, isn't your makeup heav..."

"Bye, Mom!" she interrupted her before she could finish.

Heba ran and stopped a taxi to take her to Dokki station where Ahmed was meeting her. Before she reached the station, she found him calling and answered nervously, "Hi. Yes, Ahmed. I'm almost there. Are you already at the station? Okay, I'm coming. Bye!"

Heba got out of the taxi and saw Ahmed in front of her. He smiled and asked, "How are you?"

خَمْسِين = ٥٠

مكْياج = ميْكَب *makeup*. The former word is from French and has been used for decades. The older generation and working-class people tend to use this word more. The younger, educated generation prefers words borrowed from English.

—انا تمام، اِنْتَ عامِل ايْه؟
—انا كُوَيِّس. تِحِبّ نِروح فيْن؟
—مِعرِفْش. اِخْتار اِنْتَ.
—ايْه رأيِك نِروح ناكُل مكْرونه؟ فيه واحِد كُوَيِّس بِيِعْمِل مكْرونه حِلْوَه جِدّاً قُرَيِّب.
—ماشى. اللى تِشوفُه.
—وَلّا خلّينا نِروح مكان رومانْسى اكتر. فيه **كافيْه** اعْرفُه علَى النّيل. ايْه رأيِك؟
—ماشى.

فكّرِت هِبه بِفرْحه: "مكان رومانْسى معْنَى كِده اِنُّه هَيْقولّى حاجه رومانْسيه.. يا ترَى ايْه؟"

قطع حبْل افْكارْها صوْت احمد و هُوَّ بِيِقولّها: "هِبه؟ يَلّا عشان هنْعدّى الشّارِع." و مِسِك اِيدْها. هِبه حسّت بِكْسوف و بِسعاده و عدّت معاه.

قعدوا فى الكافيْه و طلبْلها كابُتْشينو و تْشيز كيْك و طلب لِنفْسُه شاى و بصّلْها و ضِحِك.
—اِنتى هادْيَه اوى النّهارْده.
—اا..اه شُوَيّه.
—مكْسوفه عشان اوّل مرّه نُخْرُج لِوَحْدِنا؟
—اااه..

ضِحِك شُوَيّه و قالّها: "متِتِكِسْفيش اِنْتى لازِم تِتْعوّدى بقَى."
—اِتْعوّد؟

"I'm okay. How are you?"

"I'm fine. Where would you like to go?"

"I don't know. You pick."

"Okay. How about we go eat pasta? There's a guy who makes really delicious pasta near here."

"Sure. Whatever you'd like."

"Or shall we go somewhere more romantic? There's a café I know by the Nile. What do you think?"

"All right."

Heba thought happily, "Somewhere romantic? That means he will tell me something romantic. I wonder what."

Ahmed's voice interrupted her train of thought as he said, "Heba? Come on. Let's cross the street." And he took her hand. Heba felt shy and happy and crossed with him.

They sat in the café, and he ordered her a cappuccino and cheesecake, and for himself he ordered tea. He looked at her and smiled.

"You are so quiet today?"

"Ah... yeah, a little."

"Do you feel shy that we're alone for the first time?"

"Yeah."

He laughed a little and said, "Don't be shy. You should get used to it."

"Get used to it?"

كافيْه refers to modern, Western-style cafés, like *Starbucks* or the Egyptian chain *Cilantro*. The traditional, Egyptian'style coffee houses where (mostly) men gather, play backgammon, and smoke shisha are known as قَهْوَه (pl. قهاوى).

—اه..عشان اِحْنا هنُخْرُج كِتير سَوا بَعْد كِده.
—...
—عشان انا عاوِز ارْتبِط بيكى.
هِبه سِكْتِت و وِشّها احْمر و حطّت عينْها فى طبق التْشيز كيْك.
—ماشى يا سِتّى. متْقوليش حاجه دِلْوَقْتى، بسّ هسْتنَّى ردّك وَقْت ما تِحِبّى.

فِضْلِت هِبه بِتْفكّر طول الطّريق فى كلّ كِلْمه احْمد قالْها. هِىَّ مُعْجبه بيه جِدّاً بسّ خايْفه مِن خطْوة الارْتِباط. اِفْرِض اهْلها عِرْفوا وَلّا عمْرو شافْها! حاوْلِت تُطْرُد هِبه الافْكار الوِحْشه دى و تِسْتمْتِع بِريحِة برْفان احْمد اللى لِسّه فى اِيدْها.

وِصْلِت البيْت و طِلْعِت بِسعاده و اِتْرمِت علَى السّرير و فتحِت **الواتْس اب** علَى اكَوْنْت احْمد و فِضْلِت باصّه لِلصّوره و بعْديْن كتبِت:
احْمد..اَيْوَه عاوْزه نِرْتِبط. :)

و بعتِت لِصْحابْها علَى الجْروب:
بنات..بُكْره لازِم تيجوا بدْرى. فيه حاجه لازِم احْكيهالْكو!

غيّرِت هِبه هِدومْها و نامِت فى سعاده مِسْتنّيه بُكْره تِشوف احْمد تانى فى الجامْعه.

"Yeah. Because we'll go out a lot from now on."

...

"Because I want you to be my girlfriend."

Heba stayed silent, blushing, and looked down at her plate of cheesecake.

"Okay, miss. Don't say anything now. I'll wait for your response whenever you'd like."

Heba kept thinking of what he told her all the way home. She likes him a lot, but she is scared of taking the step to become his girlfriend. Suppose her parents found out, or if Amr saw her?! She tried to dismiss those bad thoughts and enjoy smelling Ahmed's cologne that was still on her hand.

She got home, happily went upstairs, lay down on her bed and opened Whatsapp on Ahmed's account and kept looking at his photo. Then she wrote, "Ahmed... Yes, I want to be your girlfriend :)"

And to her friends in the group chat, she sent, "Girls, come to the college early tomorrow. There's something I must tell you!"

Heba changed her clothes and went to bed happy, waiting for tomorrow to see Ahmed again at college.

واتْس اب *WhatsApp* is the most popular messaging app among Egyptians.

الفصْل الخامِس: تزْويغ عمْرو

"عمْرو..عمْرو..يا وَلد!"

اوّل حاجه عمْرو بيِسْمعْها فى يوْمُه، سَوا كانِت مِن مامْتُه بِنبرْه فيها مزيج مِن الزّهق و قِلِّة الحيله أوْ بِنبرْة الزّعيق و الغضب مِن والْدُه. علَى كُلّ حال عمْرو لازِم يِسْتجيب و يِقوم مِن سِريرُه رغْم اِنّها اكتر حاجه بِيِكْرهْها فى حَياتُه.

ليْه كُلّ يوْم لازِم يِتْعامِل معَ نفْس الحاجات **هِيَّ هِيَّ**: الصّحْيان بدْرى، الفِطار المُعْتاد و كوبّايِة الشّاى بلبن، الخُروج مِن البيْت بدْرى، المُواصْلات الزّحْمه، و المدْرسه، و الدُّروس...

و الكِدْب.

Chapter 5: **Amr Plays Hooky**

"Amr! Amr! Wake up, boy!"

This is the first thing Amr hears in his day, whether from his mom in a tone of boredom mixed with helplessness, or from his father in a shouting, angry tone. Either way, Amr has to respond and get out of his bed even though it is the thing he hates most in life.

Why does he have to deal with the same things every day? Waking up early, the usual breakfast with a cup of tea with milk, leaving home early, crowded public transportation, school, private lessons...

and lying.

هِيَّ هِيَّ (m. هُوَّ هُوَّ; pl. هُمَا هُمَا) *(exactly) the same*

An قَهْوَه (pl. قهاوى) is a traditional Egyptian coffee shop where locals, mostly men, enjoy beverages while smoking shisha, playing backgammon or cards, or watching soccer matches on TV.

الكِدْب بقَى حاجه يَوْميه فى حَياة عمْرو. الكِدْب انُّه راح **الدَّرْس**، انُّه مِحْتاج الفِلوس عشان الدّرْس و الملازِمِ، انُّه خلَّص مُذاكْره عشان يوافْقوا يروح القهْوَه يِشوف الماتْش و اِلىَ اخِرِه مِن الكِدْبات عشان يِفْلِت مِن ابوه و اُمُّه.

هُمَّا فى البيْت فاكْرين انُّه مِش بيرُدّ عليْهُم لمَّا بيْكلِّموه الصُّبْح عشان هُوَّ بِيْكون مقْريف مِن الصَّحَيان بدْرى، لكِن هُوَّ فى الحقيقه بِيْكون بيِفكَّر هَيْروح فيْن و هَيْقابِل مين النَّهارْده.

خرج عمْرو مِن البيْت و اِتّصل بِصاحْبُه شادى:

—ايْوَه يا صاحْبى!
—ايْوَه ياض اِزَّيَّك؟
—فيْنك كِده يا زميلى؟
—لِسَّه طالِع مِن البيْت اهو. كالعاده اُمِّى لازِم تِصحَّينى اروح المدْرسه عشان الزَّفْت **الغِياب**. اخِر مرَّه لِحِقْت **اِنْذار الغِياب** قبْل ما يُقع فى ايدْيها علىَ اخِر لحْظه.
—اه انا كمان اهْلى مِبهْدِلْنى علىَ حِوار الغِياب ده.
—طب هنِعْمِل ايْه!

Lying has become a daily habit in Amr's life. Lying that he went to the private lesson, that he needs money for the private lesson and handouts, that he finished studying so they can let him go to a coffee house and watch the match, and so on with the lies in order to get away with things without his parents knowing.

At home, they think that he doesn't reply when they talk to him in the morning because he is grumpy when he wakes up early, while in fact, he is thinking of where he will go and who he will meet today.

Amr left home and called his friend Shady.

"Hey, man!"

"Hi, how are you, buddy?"

"Where are you, my friend?"

"I just left the house. As usual, mom woke me up to go to school because of stupid attendance. Last time, I caught the attendance warning just before it would have fallen into her hands."

"Yeah, my parents are giving me grief about attendance, too."

"Then what should we do?"

دَرْس is a private lesson, one-on-one or in small groups, Egyptian students, especially those in their senior year of high school, take after school to supplement their education and prepare for tests. (A lesson/class at school is حِصّه.)

ياض is a slang form of address, mostly used between friends, but otherwise not considered polite.

غِياب (lit. *absence*) refers to *roll call* at school. اِنْذار الغِياب (lit. *absence warning*) is a notice mailed to parents whose child has had several absences and is at risk of being suspended.

—خلّينا نِروح نِحْضر كام حِصّه كِده قبْل ما ياخْدوا الغِياب و بعْدين نِزوّغ يا صاحْبى.
—طب، اِنْتَ فينْ كِده يَلّا؟
—انا هنْزِل مِن البيْت اهو.
—**قِشْطه**! هعدّى عليْك.
—مِسْتنّيك يا صاحْبى.
—سلام يا صاحْبى.

قابِل عمْرو شادى و رِكْبوا و راحوا المدْرسه قبْل يا دوْب ما يِقْفِلوا الباب. الطّابور المْمِلّ و تحيّة العلم و تمارين الصّباح اللى عمْرو مبْيِكْرهْش حاجه فى الدُّنْيا قدّها.

دخل مُدرِّس التّاريخ الفصْل:
—السّلامُ عليْكُم.
واحِد اوْ اِتْنيْن ردّ عليْه: "وَ عليْكُمُ السّلامُ."
—بِالنّسْبه لِلبهاوات اللى مبيْردّودش، مفيش اِحْتِرام!

بصّ الوِلاد كُلّ واحِد لِصاحْبُه و اللى ضِحِك. و بدأ الهمْس و الصّوْت يِعْلَى. خبط المُدرِّس علَى المكْتب بِالعصايَه علامه عن غضبُه و اِنْذار.

—النّهارْده هناخُد **الحمْله الفرنسيه علَى مصْر**. يَلّا..حدّ يِقولّى مين هُوَّ قائِد الحمْله الفرنسيه؟
صمْت و كُلُّه عامِل نفْسُه مشْغول و باصِص فى كُرّاسْتُه خايِف المُدرِّس يِخْتارُه.

"Let's go and attend a few classes until the attendance is taken and then we sneak out."

"Okay. Where are you?"

"I'm leaving the house right now."

"Okay. I'm coming to you."

"Okay. I'll wait for you, buddy."

"See you, my friend!"

Amr met Shady and they got the bus and went to school right before they closed the school gates. The boring school assembly, national anthem, and morning exercises, which Amr hates more than anything in the world.

The history teacher entered the classroom.

"As-salamu alaykum."

One or two [students] replied, "Wa alaykum as-salam."

"What about the other gentlemen who didn't reply. You have no respect!"

The kids looked at each other and some of them laughed. Whispering started and the noise became louder. The teacher hit the desk with a stick in a sign of anger and as a warning.

"Today we will learn about The French Campaign in Egypt. Okay, can anyone tell me who the leader of the French Campaign was?"

Silence. Everyone was pretending to be busy and looking at their notebooks, afraid to be picked by the teacher.

قِشْطه (lit. *cream*) is a slang expression of agreement: *okay, all right, sure.*

الحمْله الفرنسيه علَى مصْر *The French Campaign in Egypt* refers to Napoleon's attempt to conquer Egypt in the late 18 century.

—اِنْتَ..

كُلُّه رفع عيْنُه فى خوْف يِكوْن وِقِع عليْه الاخْتِيار.

—ايْوَه اِنْتَ اللى هِناك.

حطّ شادى اِيْدُه علَى صَدْرُه فى خوْف. "انا يا اُسْتاذ؟!"

—لا، اللى وَراك. اُقْعُد اِنْتَ.

قعد شادى فى ارْتِياح اِنُّه فلت.

قام عمْرو فى تَوَتُّر.

—ها يا ابْنى قول..

—اااا..مِش عارِف يا اُسْتاذ.

—مِش عارِف مين قائِد الحمْله الفرنسيه؟! اُمّال عدّيْت مِن **تالْته اِعْدادى** اِزّاى يا ابْنى؟! ده انْتو خدْتوها سِتّلاف مرّه قبْل كِده!

—انا..انا اقول يا اُسْتاذ، قال طالِب قاعِد فى الصَّفّ الاوّل.

—طبْعاً ما هُوَّ محدّش عارِف غيْر الطّلبه اللى مُجْتهِدين اللى قاعْدين فى الاوّل و قلْبُهُم علَى مصْلحِتْهُم و مُسْتقْبلْهُم، لكِن الباقى كُلُّهُم **فشله**! مِش حاسّين بِتعب ابوهُم و اُمُّهُم عشان نِفْسُهُم تِبْقوا حاجه كِبيره!

—اِبْتدينا مُحاضرات بقَى، همس شادى لِعمْرو.

—ها ها ها، ضِحك عمْرو.

—اِنْتَ يا بيْه، اِنْتَ و هُوَّ! مِش كِفايَه فشله؟ كمان بِتِتْكلِّموا معَ بعْض! اِطْلع برّه اِنْتَ و هُوَّ يَلّا!

"You."

Everyone looked up in fear that they had been picked.

"Yes, you over there."

Shady pointed his finger to his chest in fear. "Me, sir?"

"No, the one behind you. You sit."

Shady sat down, relieved that he was safe.

Amr stood up, nervous.

"Come on, son. Answer."

"Uh... I don't know, sir."

You don't know who the leader of the French Campaign was?! Then how did you make it through 9th grade, boy? You've learned about it thousands of times before!"

"I... I can answer, sir," said a student sitting in the front row.

"Of course. No one knows except the students sitting in the front who think about their future and what is best for them. But everyone else is just failing! They don't appreciate their parents' suffering hoping one day you will be someone great!"

"We've begun the lectures then!" Shady whispered to Amr.

"Ha, ha!" Amr laughed.

You there, gentlemen! Isn't it enough that you're failing? You're also talking to each other? Get out, both of you!"

تالْته اِعْدادى is the third year of middle (lit. *preparatory*) school. For more on related terms, see *Egyptian Colloquial Arabic Vocabulary (Section 10: School and Education)*.

فشله is the plural of فاشِل *failing, failure*

"يادى النّيله!" فكّر عمْرو.

خرج عمْرو و شادى وقِفوا برّه الفصْل.

—يَعْنى جينا علَى الفاضى!
—ليْه بسّ **يا صاحْبى**؟ ردّ شادى.
—اِفْرِض خدوا الغياب دِلْوَقْتى!
—لا متْخافْش **يا زميلى**. ميس ميرْفت بتاعِة الغياب بِتيجى فى الحِصّه التّانْيَه.
—يا ربّ **يا اخويا**. مِش ناقْصه هِىَّ تكْدير علَى الفاضى.

فى الحِصّه التّانْيَه دخل عمْرو و شادى الفصْل و جه مُدرِّس الدّين و قعد و قال: "مِش هنِشْرح حاجه النّهارْده بسّ كُلّه يُقْعُد ساكِت." كُلّه طلّع موبايْلُه و حطّ الهانْد فْرى فى ودانُه و شغّل مزّيكا و خلاص. شُوَيّه و دخلِت ميس ميرْفت بتاعِة الغياب و بدأوا يِكْتِبوا اسامى اللى غابوا.

اوّل ما خِلْصِت الحِصّه جرى عمْرو و شادى و كذا واحِد تانى عشان يِشوفوا فُرْصه يِزوّغوا مِن المدْرسه. و بالفِعْل، اِسْتنّوا لمّا مُشْرِف الحوْش دخل الحمّام و جِرْيوا بِسُرْعه نطّوا علَى السّور و طِلْعوا يِجْروا.

—ها ها ها! شُفْت اِزّاى فلتْنا يا صاحْبى!
ردّ عمْرو: "اِسْكُت **يا عمّ**. ده انا كُلّ مرّه بخاف نِتْقِفِش و يِبْعتوا لِابويا و اتْبِهْدِل. ده انا مُمْكِن مشوفْش الشّارِع فيها تانى دى."

"Oh, crap!" Amr thought.

Amr and Shadi went out and stood outside the classroom.

"We came here for nothing!"

"Why do you say that, man?" Shady replied.

"What if they take attendance now?"

"No, don't worry, my friend, Miss Mervat, the one responsible for taking attendance, comes in second period."

"Hopefully, bro! We can't just have gone to all this trouble for nothing."

In second period, Amr and Shady went back inside the classroom and the religion teacher came in, sat down, and said, "We aren't going to talk about anything today. Everyone sit in silence." Everyone got out their cell phones, put in their earphones, and just played music. Later, Miss Mervat, the attendance taker, came in and they started writing the names of those who were absent.

Once the class finished, Amr, Shady, and some other students ran and waited for a chance to ditch school. They waited until the yard supervisor went to the bathroom, and they ran quickly and jumped over the fence and set off running.

"Ha, ha, ha! See how we got away, man?"

Amr replied, "Shut up, man. Every time, I feel so scared of getting caught and them telling my father and I'd be screwed. I might not ever see the street again."

يا صحْبى (lit. *my friend*), يا زميلى (lit. *my colleague*), and يا اخويا (lit. *my brother*) are some of the most common forms of address used between male friends. يا عمّ (lit. *uncle*), يا ابْنى (lit. *my son*), and يا اسْطَى (lit. *boss*) are used between friends playfully or with sarcasm.

—لا يا زميلى، عدِّت اهو، متْخافْش. يَلّا هنِعْمِل ايْه دِلْوَقْتى؟
—مِش عارِف..
—تيجى نِروح عنْد **صُبْحى** بِتاع الكِبْده؟ **الواحِد** جعان.
—قِشْطه.

راحوا عنْد صُبْحى و كلوا كِبْده و مِخلِّل و سُجُقّ و قاموا.

—السّاعه تيجيلْها كام دِلْوَقْتى ياض يا شادى؟
—السّاعه دِلْوَقْتى ١٢ الضُّهْر.
—لِسّه اليوْم فى اوّلُه. ما تيجى نِدخُل سينما ياض؟
—سينما؟ اِنْتَ ضرِبْت علَى فلوس الدّرْس ولّا ايه يا صاحْبى؟
—اه، ها ها ها! اِنْتَ معْرِفْتِش تِطلّع بِمصْلحه مِن ابوك؟
—لا انا غلْبان. معايا ٢٥ جِنيْه بسّ.
—قِشْطه، هدْفعْلك انا المرّه دى عشان اِنْتَ حبيبى!
—**ربِّنا يِخلِّيك ليّا** يا اسْطَى!

—دخلوا فيلْم مُحمّد سعد الجديد و طِلْعوا وقْفوا قُدّام السِّينما. عدِّت تلات بنات حِلْوين. راح شادى صفر و قال: "احْلَى واحْده فيكو اللى لابْسه جزْمه حمْرا!" و هِىَّ مُعاكْسه هدفْها اِنَّ البنات تِبُصّ علَى جزمْها و مفيش ولّا واحْده فيهُم جزْمِتْها حمْرا اساساً.

"Nah, my friend. We're in the clear. Don't worry. Come on, what should we do now?"

"I don't know."

"What about we go to Sobhi and eat liver? I'm hungry."

"All right."

They went to Sobhi, ate liver, pickles, and sausage and then left.

"What time is it now, Shady?"

"It's 12 o'clock."

"It's still early in the day. What about we go to a movie?"

"A movie! Did you steal the private lesson fees, man?"

"Yeah. Ha, ha! Couldn't you fool your father?"

"No, I'm poor. I only have 25 pounds."

"Okay. I'll pay this time because you're my pal!"

"Thanks! You're the best!"

They saw the new Mohammed Saad movie and then went out and stood in front of the movie theater. Three beautiful girls passed by. Shady whistled and said, "You, the pretty one with the red shoes." It's a catcall that aims to make the girls look down at their shoes, even though none of them is wearing red shoes.

صُبْحى (officially مطْعم صُحْبى كابِر) is a popular Egyptian *fastfood* restaurant located between Ramses Station and Embaba Bridge.

الواحِد is used as the impersonal pronoun *one*. However, it can also be used to mean *I*, especially in situations where the speaker does not want to sound demanding.

خمْسه و عِشْرين = ٢٥؛ اِتْناشر = ١٢

ربّنا يِخلّيك (لِيّا) (lit. *May God keep you (for me)*) is an expression of gratitude, said after someone has done you a favor.

قال عمرو: "اِنْتَ اهْبل يا ابْنى؟ ثُمَّ المُعاكْسه دى قديمه جِدّاً."
—هُوَّ اِنْتَ ليه عُمرك ما بتْعاكِس يا صاحْبى؟
—مبحِبِّش الجَوّ ده، ثُمَّ انا عنْدى اُخْت بِنْت و محِبِّش حدّ يِعاكِسْها و انا اعْمِل كِده فى بنات النّاس.
—والله عِنْدك حقّ يا صاحْبى.
—ما تيجى نُقْعُد علَ **القهْوَه** نِشْربْلنا **حجرين**.
—يَلّا بينا!

قعد عمْرو علَى القهْوَه و شرِب حجر شيشه **معسِّل** هُوَّ و شادى مَع كُبّايتَيْن شاى و لعْبوا طاوْله. شُوَيّه و لقوا عِيال يعْرفوهُم داخْلين علَيْهُم. سلِّموا علَى بعْض و قعدوا علَى القهْوَه مَع بعْض، و اتْفرَّجوا علَى ماتْش ارْسنال و تْشيلْسى.

شُوَيّه و عمْرو لقَى موبايْلُه بِيرِنّ، مامْتُه بِتِتِّصِل.

—أَيْوَه يا عمْرو اِنْتَ فين كُلّ ده مِش علَى اساس درْس التّاريخ مِن ٢ ل ٤؟ السّاعه بقِت خمْسه.
—لا ما هُوَّ اصْلُه الاُسْتاذ اجِّل المعاد لِ ٤ و هخلِّص ٦ و اجى..
—ماشى سلام، خلِّ بالك مِن نفْسك!
—سلام..

فكّر عمْرو فى نفْسُه: "كِدْبه تِفوت وَلا حدّ يِموت.."

Amr said, "Are you dumb, man? That line is so old!"

"Hey, why don't you ever catcall?"

"I don't like that behavior. I have a sister and I don't like anyone pestering her, so how can I do this to other people's girls?"

"Yeah, you're right, my friend."

"Let's go to the coffee house and smoke a couple shishas."

"Let's go!"

Amr sat down at the coffee house and smoked a "honeyed" shisha, as did Shady. They drank two cups of tea and played backgammon. Later, they saw some guys they know approaching. They greeted each other and sat together in the coffee house to watch a match between Arsenal and Chelsea.

A few minutes later, Amr found his cell phone ringing. His mom was calling him.

"Hello, Amr. Where have you been all this time?! Didn't you say the history lesson was from two to four o'clock? It's five now."

"No. The teacher postponed the lesson to four o'clock, so I'll finish at six and come home."

"All right. Bye! Take care!"

"Bye!"

Amr thought to himself, "One more lie won't hurt anyone."

القهْوَه (lit. *the coffee*) is a traditional Egyptian coffee house, mostly frequented by men. (كافيْه is a modern, Western-style café.) See photograph on p. 63.

حجر (lit. *stone*) refers to the clay bowl that sits atop a shisha and holds the tobacco and coals. This word is used to count and order shishas.

معسِّل (lit. *honeyed*) refers to the type of tobacco used in shishas which can be (fruit) flavored.

الفصْل السّادِس: صديق ميدو السِّرّي

يوْم طَويل تاني..

ميدو خرج مِن المدْرسه شايل شنْطِتُه التِّقيله. علىَ رأى مامْتُه: "كانّ فيها طوب مِش كُتُب." مِشى ميدو لِحدّ محطّة الميكْروباصات كالعاده و اِسْتنَّى ميكْروباص **رمْسيس** و نِزِل فى المحطّه بتاعْتُه.

فى طريقه للبيْت ميدو شاف قُطّه صُغيِّره قاعْده لِوَحْدها جنْب الزِّباله. ميدو طِلِع مِن شنْطِتُه باقى سنْدويتْش الكُفْته اللى مامْتُه عملِتُه و حطُّه قُدَّام القُطّه. القُطّه طلَّعِت الكُفْته و فِضْلِت تاكُل فيها.

ميدو مِشى كمَّل طريقُه للبيْت و بعْديْن بصّ وَراه لقَى القُطّه ماشْيَه وَراه.

"بِتِعْمِلى ايه! اِمْشى روحى أُقْعُدى مكانِك. مامْتِك زمانْها بِتْدوّر عليْكى!

Chapter 6: **Mido's Secret Friend**

Another long day...

Mido left school carrying his heavy bag. Or, as his mom says, "as if there are rocks in there, not books." Mido walked to the microbus station as usual, waited for the Ramses microbus, and got off at his stop.

On his way home, Mido saw a kitten sitting alone next to some garbage. Mido took the rest of the kofta sandwich his mom had made him out of his bag and put it in front of the cat. The cat took out the kofta pieces and started eating.

Mido continued on his way home. And when he looked back, he found the cat following him.

"What are you doing? Go and sit where you were. Your mom might be looking for you now!"

Mido takes the microbus from his school to Ramses Station to get home. محطّة

رمْسيس *Ramses Station* is also known as محطّة مصْر (lit. *Cairo Station*). It serves as a large travel hub, with a railway station, stations for two subway lines, trams, microbuses, and taxis.

"اِمْشى بقولّك..هِش هِش!"

فِضْلِت القُطّه ماشْيَه وَراه و مِش عاوْزه تِسيبُه. ميدو شال القُطّه و حطّها فى جيْب السُّويتْشيرْت و مِشى بِسُرْعه و طِلع العِماره بِتاعْتُه.

— صباح الخيرْ يا اُسْتاذ ميدو." صوْت عمّ احْمد **البوّاب**.
ميدو مِن غيْر ما يْبُصّ: "اااا.. الحمْدُ لله."
— اِنْتَ كُوَيِّس..؟
— اااا..ہا..

قبْل ما يِلْحق ميدو يِجْرى يِطْلع السِّلّم القُطّه نطّت مِن جِيْبُه.

— الله! قُطّه صُغيّرْه! بابا اِشْتراهالك؟
— لا لا، ميدو بارْتِباك.
— ...
— انا اكِّلْتها سنْدويتْش الكُفْته بِتاعى و هِيَّ اللى مِشْيِت وَرايا و بِعْدِت عن بيْتها و لَوْ سِبْتها هتوه اوْ..اوْ كلْب هَياكُلْها اوْ عربيه هتْدوسْها اوْ..
عمّ احْمد بِيْقاطْعُه: "تمام تمام! وَلا يِهِمّك يا اُسْتاذ ميدو."

"Go! Shoo, shoo!"

The cat kept following him and didn't want to leave him. Mido picked the cat up, put it in his sweatshirt pocket, walked quickly, and went inside his apartment building.

"Good morning, Mr. Mido!" It was Mr. Ahmed, the building's doorman.

Mido, without looking, said, "Ah... I'm fine, thanks."

"Are you okay?"

"Yeah, yeah."

Before Mido could run up the stairs, the cat jumped out of his pocket.

"Oh! A little kitten! Did your dad buy you it?"

"No, no," said Mido nervously.

...

"I fed her my kofta sandwich, and she followed me away from her home. If I had left her, she would have gotten lost. Or... or a dog would have eaten her. Or a car would have run her over."

Mr. Ahmed interrupted, "Okay, okay! No worries, Mr. Mido."

بوّاب – Most buildings in Egypt employ a بوّاب (*doorman, super-intendent*), who lives in a simple apartment on the ground floor. His responsibilities include maintenance, cleaning, and guarding the building. He will also run errands, wash cars, and do other odd jobs for the occupants.

—مُمْكِن..مُمْكِن متقولْش لحدّ؟
—ماشى! هَيبْقَى سرّنا الصُّغيّر يا أُستاذ ميدو متخافْش.
—شُكراً، ميدو وَطِّى و خد القُطّه رجّعْها جيبُه.

خبط ميدو علَى باب البيْت فى خوْف و اوّل ما مامتُه فتحِت الباب جِرى بِسُرْعه دخل.

—ميدو..؟ اِنْتَ كُوَيِّس يا حبيبى؟
—اه يا ماما، انا بسّ مزْنوق و عاوِز ادخُل الحمّامِ.
—ماشى..

جِرى ميدو و طلّع القُطّه و حطّها فى كرْتونه جنب سريرُه.

—انا هسمّيكى بوسى. مُمْكِن متِعْمِليش صوْت؟
القُطّه بِتبُصّ حَوالِيْها.
—ماشى.. انا هروح دِلْوَقْتى اتْغدّى و هاجى تانى..
—...
—اِنْتى جعانه؟ وَلّا سنْدِويتْش الكُفْته لِسّه مِشبّعِك؟
—...
—طب انا هشوف و اجيلِك. خلّيكى هِنا..

طِلع ميدو و قفل الباب وَراه و بعْديْن راح المطْبخ. سِمِع احلَى صوْت بِيْحِبُّه، صوْت زيْت القلى السُّخْن و ريحِة البطاطِس و البانيْه.

"Can you please not tell anyone?"

"All right! That will be our little secret, Mr. Mido. Don't worry."

"Thank you." Mido bent over, took the cat, and put her back in his pocket.

Mido knocked on the door of his house scared. As soon as his mom opened the door he ran in.

"Mido? Are you okay, honey?"

"Yes, mom! I've just got to pee.I want to go to the bathroom."

"All right."

Mido quickly got the cat out of his pocket and put her into a box made of cardboard next to his bed.

"I'll call you Bosy. Can you please not make any noise?"

The cat was looking around.

"Okay. I'll go have lunch now, then I'll be back."

...

"Are you hungry? Or did that kofta sandwich fill you up?"

...

"All right. I'll go see, then I'll come back. Stay here."

Mido went out, shut the door behind him, and went to the kitchen. He heard the sound he likes most. The sound of hot frying oil and the smell of fries and fried chicken fillets.

—ماما..اِنْتى عامْله بطاطِس و بانِيه؟
—أَيْوَه يا حبيبى و مكْرُوْنه بِصلْصه.
—هيييْه!
—ها ها غسلْت اِيدك بعْد ما دخلْت الحمّام؟
اِفْتكر ميدو اِنُّه اصْلاً مدخلْش الحمّام. االا هروح اهو!
—ماشى.

غسل ميدو اِيدُه و راح قعد علىَ السُّفْره و مامْتُه حطّت قُدّامُه الاكْل. دى تُعْتبر اكْلِة ميدو المُفضّله.

—ماما..عنْدنا كاتْشب؟
—ثَوانى، هجيبْلك حبيبى!

خد ميدو الكاتْشب و فِضِل ياكُل و بعْديْن خد حِتّة بانِيه و خبّاها و قام.

—شِبِعْت خلاص؟
—اه الحمْدُ لله.
—ماشى، اِغْسِل اِيديْك و يَلّا عشان نِعْمِل الواجِب.
—حاضِر.

—بوسى..بوسى.. رُحْتى فيْن؟ ميدو اِتْخضّ و لقَى الكرْتوْنه فاضْيَه و مِش لاقى القُطّه. بصّ تحْت السِّرير و وَرا الكراسى. رُحْتى فيْن؟

—ميدوووو.. صاحْبك على علىَ التِّليفوْن!

"Mom, are you making French fries and fried chicken fillets?"

"Yes, honey, and pasta with tomato sauce."

"Hurray!"

"Ha, ha! Did you wash your hands after you went to the bathroom?"

Mido remembered that he didn't go to the bathroom in the first place. "Uh... I'll go now!"

"Okay."

Mido washed his hands and went to sit at the table while his mom put the food in front of him. This is Mido's favorite meal.

"Mom, do we have ketchup?"

"Just a moment. I'll bring it to you, honey."

Mido took the ketchup and started eating. Then he took one piece of fried chicken fillet, hid it, and got up.

"Are you full?"

"Yes."

"Okay. Wash your hands and let's start doing your homework."

"Right away."

"Bosy... Bosy... Where are you? Mido panicked and found the box empty and couldn't see the cat anywhere. He looked under the bed and behind the chairs. Where are you?"

"Mido! Your friend Ali is on the phone!"

—حاضِر حاضِر! بِخوْف.

حطّ مِيدو حِتّة البانِيْه علَى الكَرْتونه و طِلع مِيدو و قفل الباب وَراه و هُوَّ مُتَوَتِّر. فيْن مُمْكِن تِكون راحِت القُطّه دى.

—الو؟
—اَيْوَه يا مِيدو كُنْت عاوِز اسْألك واجِب الرِّياضِيّات علينْا ايْه؟
—ثَوانى، هروح اشوفْلك.

فتح مِيدو باب الاوْضه بِراحه و دخل يِطلّع الكشْكوْل مِن شنْطِتُه. لقَى القُطّه بِتاكُل البانِيْه. "اوْعى تِتحرّكى مِن هِنا تانى! هاجى بِسُرْعه! سامْعه؟"

رِجِع مِيدو مِسِك سمّاعِة التِّليفوْن:
—اَيْوَه يا على.
—اَيْوَه.
الواجِب صفْحه ٣١ و ٣٢.
ماشى شُكْراً.
سلام.

رِجِع مِيدو الاوْضه بِسُرْعه و اِتْأكَّد اِنّ القُطّه لِسّه مكانْها عِنْد الكرْتونه. "شطوره! هروح احُطِّلك مِيّه و اجى."

"Okay! Coming!" He was scared.

Mido put the fried chicken in the box, went out, and closed the door behind him, nervous. Where could that cat have gone?

"Hello?"

"Hi, Mido! I wanted to ask you what our math homework was for today."

"Hold on. I'll go check."

Mido opened the door of the room slowly and entered to get his notebook out of his bag. He found the cat eating the chicken. "Don't you dare go anywhere again! I'll be right back! Hear me?"

Mido went back and picked up the phone.

"Ali?"

"Yes?"

"The homework is page 31 and 32."

"Okay. Thanks!"

"Bye!"

Mido quickly went back to his room and made sure the cat was still in the box. "Good girl! I'll go get you some water."

واحِد و تلاتين و اتْنيْن و تلاتين = ٣١ و ٣٢

راح ميدو جاب عِلْبة زبادى فاضْيه و حطّ فيها ميّه. و هُوَّ رايح الاوْضه مامْتُه شافِتُه.

—هتِعْمِل ايْه بالميّه دى؟
—اااا..حاجه للواجِب..لِواجِب الـ ..الـ..
—العُلوم؟ هتِزْرعوا بصله؟
—ايْوَه! قال بسعاده زَىّ اللى لقَى فُرْصه.
—طب، اِسْتنَّى هدِّيلك بصله صُغيِّره.

خد ميدو البصله الصُّغيِّره و راح اوضْتُه. "شُكْراً!"

دخل ميدو و حطّ البصله فى الدُّرْج و رِجِع حطّ عِلْبة الميّه قُدّام القُطّه. شِرْبِت القُطّه و فِضِل ميدو يمِدّ إيدُه خايف يطبْطب عليْها و بعْديْن اِتْشجّع و لمسْها. طِلْعِت طريه و ناعْمه.

—طيِّب. اِنْتى دِلْوَقْتى كلْتى و شِرِبْتى. مُمْكِن بقَى متِعْمليش صوْت عشان عمرو زمانُه جاىّ؟ و لَوْ اِتْقفشْنا هتِرْجعى الشّارِع و مِش هعْرف اشوفِك تانى. اِتّفقْنا؟
—مياااو..
—طيِّب. هعْتِبِر ده اوكيْه بسّ متِعْمليش كِده تانى لحْسن حدّ يِسْمع.

—ميدوووو! يا وَلد يَلّا عشان نِعْمِل الواجِبات! نادِت أُمّ عمرو علَى ميدو.

Mido went and got an empty yogurt container and put water in it. As he was going back to his room, his mom saw him.

"What are you going to do with that water?"

"Uh... it's for homework. Homework for... for..."

"Science? Are you growing an onion?"

"Yes!" he said, so happy to have found this chance.

"All right. Wait. I'll give you a small onion."

Mido took the small onion and went to his room. "Thanks!"

Mido went into the room, put the onion in a drawer, and put the water box in front of the cat. The cat drank and Mido kept reaching his hand out, afraid to pet her, but then he worked up the courage and petted her. Her fur was soft.

"Okay. Now you've had something to eat and drink. Can you please not make any sound? Amr will be here at any moment. And if he catches us, you'll be back on the street and I'll never see you again. Deal?"

Meow...

"Okay. I'll take that as a yes, but don't do that again or someone will hear."

"Midooo! Come here so we can do your homework," Om Amr called Mido.

—حاضِر يا ماما، جايّ!

جاب ميدو شنْطِتُه و قعد جنْب مامْتُه.

—خدْت واجِبات ايْه النّهارْده؟
—رِياضِيّات و عربى.
—ماشى. فيه حاجه صعْبه واقْفه معاك؟
—لا كُلّه تمامِ.
—طب يلّا حِلّ و وَرّينى لوْ حاجه وقِفْت معاك.
—ماشى.

دخلِت أُمّ عمْرو الحمّام تِطلّع الغسيل مِن الغسّاله عشان تُنْشُرُه. شُوَيّة و خبط الباب.

—ميدووو..شوف مين علَى الباب عشان بنْشُر الغسيل!
—حاضِر!

فتح ميدو الباب، لقَى عمْرو.

—عمْرو! قال بِخوْف و مُفاجْأه.
—ما لك ياض؟ زَيّ ما تِكون شُفْت عِفْريت!
—لا! انا بسّ افْتكرْتك عنْدك درْس.
—اه بسّ السّاعه خمْسه. رِجِعْت البيْت اخُد شاوَر و اتْغدَّى. فيه حاجه؟!

"Coming, mom!"

Mido brought his bag and sat next to his mom.

"What homework do you have today?"

"Math and Arabic."

"All right. Is there anything you're having trouble with?"

"No. it's all fine."

"Okay. Start doing the homework and let me know if you find anything difficult."

"Okay."

Om Amr went to the bathroom to get the laundry out of the washing machine to hang it out to dry. Then there was a knock at the door.

"Midooo! See who's at the door. I'm hanging up the laundry."

"Okay!"

Mido opened the door to find Amr.

"Amr!" he said, surprised and scared.

"What is it? You look like you've seen a ghost!"

"No! I just thought you had a private lesson."

"Yes, but at five. I came home to shower and have lunch. Do you have a problem!?"

—لا مفيش طبْعاً.

جِرى ميدو بِسُرْعه لِلأوْضه عُقْبال ما عمْرو دخل الحمّام. و مِسِك الكرْتونه.

"بوسى! عمْرو هَيِدْخُل **ناو**. متْخافيش. ده اخويا الكِبير، ماشى؟ اِوْعى تِعْمِلى صوْت."

خبَّى الكرْتونه تحْت السَّرير، عمْرو فتح الباب فى اللَّحْظه دى.

—بِتِعْمِل ايه يا وَله؟
—مفيش. بدوَّر على حاجه ضاعِت مِنّى.
—طيِّب... يَلّا اِطْلع شُوَيّة عشان هتْكلِّم فى الموبايْل.
—ايه..بسّ انا..هقْعُد هِنا مِن غيْر ما اعْمِل صوْت..
اِنْتَ هتْهزَّر؟

خرج ميدو و هُوَّ خايف جِدّاً عمْرو يِلاقى القُطَّه و يقول لِمامْتُه. ميدو مِن زمان نِفْسُه فى قُطَّه أوْ كلْب أوْ حتَّى عصْفور بسّ مامْتُه مِش بِتْحِبّ الحيَوانات الاليفه.

طِلِع ميدو قعد جنْب مامْتُه قُدّام التِّلِفِزْيوْن و هُوَّ خايِف و مُتَوَتِّر.

فى الوَقْت ده عمْرو كان بِيتْكلِّم فى الموبايْل و قاعِد فجْأه حسّ حاجه بِتِلْمِس رِجْلُه. عمْرو اِتْخضّ و اِتْنفض.

"No, of course not."

Mido ran to his room while Amr was in the bathroom and held the box.

"Bosy! Amr is coming in now. Don't be scared. He's my big brother, okay? Don't make any sound."

No sooner had he hid the box under the bed than Amr opened the door.

"What are you doing, kid?"

"Nothing. I'm looking for something I lost."

"Okay.... Now, go out for a while because I'm going to make a call."

"What? I'll just stay here and not make any sound."

"Are you kidding me?"

Mido left the room so scared that Amr would find the cat and tell his mom. For a long time, Mido has wanted to have a cat or a dog, or even a bird, but his mom doesn't like pets.

Mido went and sat next to his mom in front of the TV, scared and nervous.

Meanwhile, Amr was sitting, talking on the phone when he suddenly felt something touching his foot. Amr got scared and jumped up.

ناو is the English word *now*. It is common among educated Egyptians to sprinkle English words into everyday speech.

مياو! مياو!

"اِنْتى جيتى مِنيْن! بِسْمِ الله الرّحْمن الرّحيم!"

عمْرو شال القُطّه و طِلِع الصّاله.

—مامااااا.. فيه قُط..
ميدو قاطْعُه بِسُرْعه: "أيّوَه أيّوَه، انا جِبْتها. مُمْكِن مَتْقولْش لِماما عشان خاطْرى لَوْ سمحْت؟"
—اِنْتَ اِتْجنّنْت. اكيد هتِسْمع صوتْها أوْ و اِنْتَ فى المدْرسه و هِيَّ بِتْنضّف الاوْضه هتْلاقيها.
—ارْجوك يا عمْرو!
—مِش هَيِنْفع **يا عمرّ**! لازِم تِطْلعْها برّه البيْت. لا تِطْلع مِش نضيفه و تِجيبْلك امْراض!
—طيِّب خلاص خلاص، انا هاخُدْها.
—ماشى.

خد ميدو الكرْتونْه و اِتْسحب برّه.

—ماما..انا هنْزِل اجيب كرّاسه مِن المكْتبه.
—معاك فِلو...؟ قبْل ما تِخلّص الجُمْله ميدو كان نِزِل و قفل الباب.

Meow! meow!

"Where did you come from? My God!"

Amr picked up the cat and went out to the living room.

"Mom! There's a ca…"

Mido quickly interrupted him. "Yes, yes. I'm the one who brought her. Can you please not tell mom for me? Please?"

"You're crazy! She's for sure going hear her make noise. Or when you're at school and she is cleaning, she'll find her."

"Please, Amr!'

"No way, kid! You have to get her out of the house. What if she's not clean and gives you a disease?"

"All right, all right! I'll do it."

"Okay."

Mido took the box and sneaked outside.

"Mom, I'm going to buy a notebook from the stationery shop."

"Do you have mon…" Before she could finish the sentence, Mido was already gone and had closed the door.

يا عمّ (lit. *uncle*) and يا ابْنى (lit. *my* son) can be used mockingly.

ميدو و هُوَّ زعْلان شافهُ عمّ احْمد.

—ما لك يا أُسْتاذ ميدو؟
—عمْرو لقَى القُطّه و قالَّ لازِم امشّيها لَهَيقول لماما.
—طب. ايْه رأيُك يا أُسْتاذ ميدو اخلّيها عنْدى و تيجى تِلْعب معاها فى حوْش البيْت كُلّ يوْم بعْد المدْرسه؟
—بِجدّ؟ شُكْراً يا عمّ احْمد!
—وَلا يِهِمّك يا أُسْتاذ ميدو..ده هَيِبْقَى سِرّنا الصُّغيّر..

Mr. Ahmed saw Mido looking sad.

"What's wrong, Mr. Mido?"

"Amr found the cat and said I had to get rid of her or he would tell mom."

"Okay. What if I keep her with me and you come play with her every day after school in the yard of the building?"

"Really? Thanks, Mr. Ahmed!"

"Don't worry, Mr. Mido. It'll be our little secret."

لَ + bare imperfect or future verb is synonymous with لحْسن *lest, or else, or otherwise; for fear that…*

الفصْل السّابِع: الازْمه

"يا سيِّد.."

بدأ ابو عمْرو يِفوق و ياخُد بالُه مِن صوْت اُمّ عمْرو.

—يا سيِّد اِنْتَ كُوَيِّس؟ مِش هتْروح تِفْتح الصَّيْدليه النّهارْده وَلّا ايْه؟
—قُمْت اهو خلاص.
—صباح الخيْر. اعْمِلّك بيْض مقْلى وَلّا مسْلوق؟
—مقْلى..
—ماشى.

قام ابو عمْرو حاسِس اِنُّه تعْبان و **قلْبُه مقْبوض**. يا ترَى مَيفْتحْش الصَّيْدليه النّهارْده و يِريَّح شُوَيّه قُدّام التِّلفِزْيوْن. "اكيد هزْهق. خلِّينى انْزِل و اشغَّل الرّادْيو الصُّغيِّر اللى فى الصَّيْدليه و خلاص.." قال ابو عمْرو لِنفْسُه.

Chapter 7: **The Crisis**

"Hey, Sayed!"

Abu Amr started to wake up and pay attention to Om Amr's voice.

"Sayed, are you okay? Aren't you going to work at the pharmacy today?"

"Okay, I'm up."

"Good morning! Do you want fried or boiled eggs?"

"Fried."

"Okay."

Abu Amr got up feeling tired and that something bad was going to happen. Should he just not go to the pharmacy today and relax in front of the TV instead? "I'll definitely feel bored. I'll just go and play the small radio at the pharmacy," Abu Amr said to himself.

قلْبُه مقْبوض (lit. one's heart is clutched) with a sense of foreboding

قعد علَ الطّربيْزه و فِطِر و شِرِب كُبّايةِ الشّاى.

—هقوم انا، اتّكِل علَ الله.
—معَ السّلامه...بقولّك صحيح يا ابو عمْرو!
"مادام نادِتْنى ابو عمْرو يبْقَى هتُطْلُب حاجه كِبيره،" فكّر ابو عمْرو فى نفْسُه.
—خيْر؟
—لَو عِرِفْت تجيبْلنا لحْمه يا ريْت. العِيال بقالُهُم كِتير اوى مكلوهاش.

سِكِت ابو عمْرو. اللّحْمه غِلْيِت اوى زَىّ كُلّ حاجه فى البلد. و الصّيْدليه بعْد زيادةِ الضّرايب و الجمارِك و منْع ادْويه كِتيره مِسْتوْرده مبقِتْش ماشْيه كُوَيِّس زَىّ الاوّل. النّاس بقى عندها اِسْتِعْداد تِسْتحْمِل الالم وَلا اِنّها تِدْفع كُلّ ده فى بِرْشامةِ صُداع وَلّا برْد.

خرج ابو عمْرو و مِشى فى الشّارِع باصِص حَوالِيْه علَ البيّاعين البُسطا و النّاس الغلابه و فكّر: "اِزّاى النّاس دى عايْشه فى الغلا ده كُلُّه؟"

—صباح الخير يا **دُكتور** سيّد! صاحِب البِقاله اللى قُدّامُه قالُه و هُوَّ شايْفه بيِفْتح الصّيْدليه.
—صباح النّور يا عمّ اِبْراهيم. ايْه اخْبارك؟

He sat down at the table to have breakfast and drink a cup of tea.

"I'm going now."

"Goodbye! Ah, I wanted to ask you for something, Abu Amr!"

"She called me Abu Amr, so she must be about to ask for something big," Abu Amr thought to himself.

"What is it?"

"If you could bring us some meat, that would be great. The children haven't had any in so long."

Abu Amr didn't say anything. The price of meat had gone up so much, just like everything in the country. And after tax increases, customs duty, and prohibitions on many imported drugs, the pharmacy wasn't doing as well as in the past. People had become inclined to bearing pain rather than pay for cold or headache pills.

Abu Amr left home and walked down the street looking around at the modest vendors and poor people and thought, "How are these people living with these crazy price increases?"

"Good morning, Dr. Sayed!" the grocer in front of his pharmacy said to him when he saw him opening the pharmacy.

"Good morning, Mr. Ibrahim. How are you?"

يا ابو عمرو – Married couples normally call each other by their first names. Here, Om Amr is trying to sound more polite and formal, as she asks for a favor, as Abu Amr suspects.

خيْر؟ (I hope it is something) good?, said in jest.

دُكتور – The title دُكتور is extended to pharmacists in Egypt, even though they do not have doctorate degrees.

بِسُرْعه نِدِم ابو عمرو علىَ سُؤالُه ده عشان عمّ اِبْراهيم فتح فى الكلام و الشَّكْوَى مِن زِيادة اسْعار كُلّ حاجه. و اِزّاى كُلّ ما بيجى يِشْترى بِضاعه يِلاقى مكسبُه مِن الشُّحْنه اللى قبْلها معادش يِكَفَّى لِلكَمِّيات الجِديده. و اِزّاى كُلّ الزَّباين مِضايْقين مِنُّه زَىّ ما يِكون ذنبُه الغلا اللى صايب البلد.*

—كان الله فى العوْن، ربَّنا يوَسَّع علينا كُلَّنا، قال ابو عمرو و هُوَّ بيْحاوِل يِقْفِل فى الكلام و فتح الصَّيْدليه و دخل و قفل الباب وَراه.

يوْم ابو عمرو بيْعدَّى بِبُطء شديد. مِشغَّل الرَّادْيو و بيخْدِم زبونين تلاته فى اليوْم بـ ٢٠ لِ ٥٠ جِنيْه. بعْدين بيِرْجع البيْت يِتْغدَّى و يِريَّح شُوَيّه و يرْجع يِفْتح تانى شِفْت باللّيْل و برْضُه بييجيلُه عميلين تلاته.

بعْد ما رِجِع و هُوَّ قاعِد بيِتْغدَّى حسّ نفْس اِحْساس اِنّ قلْبُه مقْبوض و مِش حابِب يِروح الصَّيْدليه.

"مجبْتِلْناش لحْمه يَعْنى؟" قطعِت عليْه أمّ عمرو حبل افْكارُه و كاِنَّها بِتْقولُّه فِكْرة يِنْسىَ اِنُّه يِريَّح قُدَّام التِّلِفِزْيوْن و اِنَّهُم مِحْتاجين فِلوس.

Abu Amr immediately regretted his question, as Mr. Ibrahim went on and on complaining about the price increases of everything. And how every time he goes to buy merchandise, he finds that what he made out of previous sales is not enough to buy new quantities. And how all customers are so mad at him, as if the price increases that had hit the country were his fault.

"May God help us and bless us all," Abu Amr said trying to put and end to the talk. He opened the pharmacy, went inside, and closed the door behind him.

Abu Amr's day goes very slowly. He plays the radio, serves a couple of customers over the day for 20 to 50 pounds. Then he goes home to have lunch and take a rest. Then he goes back again for the evening shift. And, like during the day, two or three customers come.

When he had gone home to have lunch, he felt the same feeling that something bad would happen and that he didn't want to go back to the pharmacy.

"You didn't buy us meat, then?" Om Amr brought him back to reality as if she was telling him to forget about resting in front of the TV and that they needed money.

---

*In late 2016, Egypt took a $12 billion loan from the IMF, a condition for which was floating the Egyptian pound. This caused it to lose half of its value overnight and resulted in high inflation. The economic struggles Egyptians are facing in these difficult times are illustrated in this and the following chapter.

بِعِشْرين لِخَمْسين = بِ ٢٠ لِ ٥٠

—... نسيت.
—وَلا يِهمّك. طب ما تِجيبْلنا مِن عمّ عبْدُه الجزّار و اِنْتَ راجِع باللّيْل؟ نِعْمِلّنا بُكْره طاجِن بِمّيَه وَلّا حاجه.
—اِن شاء الله.

خرج ابو عمْرو و هُوَّ مشْغول البال. و قعد فى الصَّيْدليه معدّاش ساعه و لقَى واحِد شابّ داخِل عليْه مِن اللى شكْلُهُم معْروف بالنِّسْبالُه. شعْر واقِف، سلْسِله، بنْطلون ساقِط، سمّاعه فى ودْنُه. عادةً بِيبْقوا عاوْزين جِل لِشعْرُهُم.

—أيْوَه يا ابْنى، اِتْفضّل.
—عاوِز سِرِنْجات.
—معاك روشِتّه؟
—لا.

ابو عمْرو بدأ يِتْوَتّر. ممْنوع صرْف سِرِنْجات مِن غيْر روشِتّه. ابو عمْرو عارِف اِنّ السِّرِنْجات دى هتِسْتخْدِم فى ضرْب المُخدّرات و مِش مُمْكِن يِتْوَرّط فى حاجه زَىّ كِده.

—والله يا ابْنى، ممْنوع اصرِفْلك سِرِنْجات مِن غيْر روشِتّه.
—مُتأكّد يَعْنى؟ اخِر كلام؟

اِتْوَتّرِت ملامِح ابو عمْرو و لمح طرف المطْوَه اللى طلّعُه الشابّ مِن جيْبُه و قرّبُه ناحْية ابو عمْرو.

"I forgot."

"It's okay. What about you buy us some from Abdu the butcher on your way home in the evening? We can make some okra casserole or something tomorrow."

"God willing."

Abu Amr left home worried. He hadn't been back at the pharmacy even an hour when a young man came in who had a look familiar to Abu Amr: spiky hair, a chain, sagging pants, headphones on. Normally these types want gel for their hair.

"Hi! How can I help you, young man?"

"I need syringes."

"Do you have a prescription?"

"No."

Abu Amr started to tense up. It's forbidden to give out syringes without a prescription. Abu Amr knew well that these syringes would be used to do drugs and he couldn't get involved in something like that.

"I swear, young man, it's forbidden to give you syringes without a prescription."

"Are you sure? Is that your final answer?"

Abu Amr's face tensed up as he saw the blade of the pocket knife the young man had pulled out of his pocket and put close to Abu Amr.

—اِدّينى السِّرِنْجات دِلْوَقْتى.
بِخوْف طلّع باكِت سِرِنْجات و ادّاه لِلشّابّ.
—واحِد تانى بِسُرْعه!!
طلّع الكِيس التّانى و ادّاهولُه.

الوَلد عيْنُه راحِت لِلكاشير و فكّر: "طالما اِدّانى اللى انا عاوْزُه ما اخُد فِلوس كمان."

—اِفْتح الكاشير!
—ايْه؟
—اِفْتح بِسُرْعه بقولّك!
فتح ابو عمْرو و لِلاسف كان فيه فِلوس فى الخزْنه و اللى هُوَّ بِياخُدْها يِشيلْها البنْك اخِر الاِسْبوع.
—**اِعْمِل معْروف** يا ابْنى!
—هات يلّا بِسُرْعه!

فى اللّحْظه دى عمّ اِبْراهيم البقّال عدّى مِن قُدّام الصَّيْدليه:
—يلّا بينا يا دُكْتور سيِّد. اِنْتَ لِسّه قاعِد شُوَيّه ولّا ايْه؟

بصّ الشّابّ لِابو عمْرو و قرّب السِّكينه اكْتر و شاوِرْلُه يِرُدّ بِهُدوء.

—اااه..اااه انا هقْعُد كمان شُوَيّه. اِتِّكِل اِنْتَ علَى الله!

"Give me the syringes now."

Scared, he took a package of syringes and gave it to the young man."

"Another one, quickly!!"

He took another one and gave it to him.

The young man looked to the cashier and thought, "If he gave me what I wanted, then I will take money, as well."

"Open the cash register!"

"What!"

"I said open it, quick!"

Abu Amr opened it, and unfortunately, there was money in the drawer which he takes to deposit at the bank at the end of the week.

"Please, young man!"

"Give me it, quick!"

At this moment Mr. Ibrahim, the grocer, passed in front of the pharmacy.

"Let's go, Dr. Sayed. Are you staying for a while more or what?"

The young man looked at Abu Amr and put the knife closer and gestured to him to respond quietly.

"Uh... yes, I'm staying for a little bit. You can go ahead.

اِعْمِل مَعْروف *Please!* is an expression of begging for mercy or a special favor.

اِتِّكِل عَلَى الله (lit. *Trust in God!*) is used to tell someone to go ahead (without you) or, to beggars, to go away. (See also note on p. 127.)

مدّ الشابّ إيدُه فى الكاشير و خد كبْشة فِلوس و جِرى بِسُرْعه. قعد ابو عمْرو علَى الكُرْسى ياخُد نفْسُه مِن التّوَتُّر.

"لا حَوْلَ وَ لا قُوَّه اِلَّا بِالله. اِنَّا لله وَ اِنَّا اِلَيْهِ راجِعون."

قفل ابو عمْرو الصّيْدليه و رِجِع البيْت مهْموم و مغْموم. فتحِت اُمّ عمْرو الباب و اوِّل ما شافتُه عِرْفِت اِنّ فيه حاجه غلط.

—خيْر يا ابو عمْرو، ما لك؟

مردِّش و دخل اوضْتُه غيْر هِدومُه و نام فى سِريرُه. شُوَيّه و جت اُمّ عمْرو تانى دخلِت عليْه الاوْضه.

—ابو عمْرو؟ ما لك؟ اِنْتَ كُوَيِّس؟

مردِّش عليْها و عمل نفْسُه نايِم.

—اِنْتَ نِمْت خلاص؟ **ربَّنا يُسْتُر يا ربّ، يا ربّ جيب العَواقِب سليمه.**

خرجِت اُمّ عمْرو و قفلِت عليْه باب الاوْضه.

The young man put his hands in the cash register, got a handful of money, and quickly ran off. Abu Amr sat down on his chair to catch his breath from panic.

"There is no power except in God. We belong to God and to Him we will go back."

Abu Amr closed the pharmacy and went home, sad and worried. Om Amr opened the door, and as soon as she saw him, she realized there was something wrong.

"What is wrong, Abu Amr?!"

He didn't answer and went to his room, changed his clothes and went to bed. A few minutes later, Om Amr came in the room.

"Abu Amr? What happened? Are you okay?"

He didn't reply and pretended to be asleep.

"Are you already asleep? Oh, dear God, protect us and save us from any trouble."

Om Amr went out and closed the door of the room.

اِنّا لله وَ اِنّا اِلَيْهِ راجِعـون and لا حَوْلَ وَ لا قُوّه اِلّا بِالله are two formulaic expressions from Classical Arabic, which can be uttered after experiencing, witnessing, or hearing about a bad situation. They imply that the situation is in God's hands and that you accept his will (your fate). The first expression is more common and can be used alone, while the second is only used in quite serious situations.

رِبَّنا يُسْتُرْ يا رِبّ، يا رِبّ جيب العَواقِب سليمه are also formulaic expressions uttered in a troubling situation.

فِضِل ابو عمْرو مِش قادِر يِنام و مهْموم. مِش كِفايَه اِنُّه خِسِر قيمِة كيسيْن سرْنِجات لكِن كمان خد كُلّ فِلوس جابْها فى الاِسْبوع ده. هَيِعْمِل ايْه دِلْوَقْتى؟ بُكْره بيجى عمْرو يِقولُّه: "هات فلوس الدّرْس." و هِبه تقولُّه: "يا بابا عاوْزه فِلوس اجيب لِبْس حِلْو زَىّ صاحْباتى." و ميدو يِفْضل يِشْتِكى: "يا بابا المصْروف مِش كِفايَه." و اُمّ عمْرو! اُمّ عمْرو هتِفْضل تِقولُّه: "عاوْزين لحْمه، عاوْزين فاكْهه، عاوْزين فِلوس كِسْوِة العيد، عاوْزين..عاوْزين..."

حسّ ابو عمْرو اِنّ ضغْطُه بيِعْلى عليْه و قلْبُه بيْدُقّ بِسُرْعه. و نادَى: "يا سامْيَه! يا سامْيَه!"

دخلِت اُمّ عمْرو مخْضوضه.

—ما لك يا سيِّد؟ اِنْتَ كُوَيِّس؟ خضّيتْنى عليْك!
—هاتيلى دَوا الضغْط بِتاعى و كوبّاية ميّه.
—حاضِر..حاضِر..
خرجِت اُمّ عمْرو بِسُرْعه فى خوْف و جابِت الدَّوا و الميّه و قعدِت جنْبُه ناوْلِتُه الحاجه. خدِت مِنُّه الكوبّايَه بعْد ما شِرِب.

—ما لك بسّ؟ مِش هتْقولّى ايْه اللى حصل؟ اِنْتَ مِن ساعِة ما رِجِعْت و اِنْتَ شكْلك فيك حاجه؟
—مفيش حاجه يا سامْيَه. سيبينى لِوَحْدى.
—حاجه حصلِت فى الشُّغْل طيِّب؟

Abu Amr stayed in bed, unable to sleep and worried. Not only did he lose the value of two packages of syringes, but the guy also took all the money he made that week. What was going to do now? Amr will come and ask him for the private lesson tuition. Heba will say to him, "Dad, I want money to buy nice clothes, like my friends." Mido will keep complaining, "Dad, my pocket money is not enough." And Om Amr! Om Amr will keep saying, "We need meat. We need fruit. We need money for holiday outfits. We want... want..."

Abu Amr felt his blood pressure increasing and his heart beating fast. He called, "Samia! Samia!"

Om Amr came in, scared.

"What is wrong, Sayed? Are you okay? You scared me!"

"Bring me my blood pressure medicine and a glass of water."

"Right away."

Om Amr went out in a hurry and brought the medicine and the water and sat next to him handing them to him. She took the glass after he had finished drinking.

"What is it? You won't tell me what happened? Since you came home, you've looked like there's something wrong."

"It's nothing, Samia. Leave me alone!"

"Did something happen at work then?"

—مفيش حاجه.
—قولّ طيِّب. قلقْتِني عليْك!
—يوووه يا سامْيَه! مفيش حاجه قُلْت!

خرجِت أُمّ عمْرو مهْمومه و زعْلانه. زَيّ كُلّ الرِّجاله ابو عمْرو عُمْرُه ما بِيحْكيلْها اَيّ حاجه مِضايْقاه.

فكَّر ابو عمْرو فى نفْسُه: "انا عارِف اِنّها بتِزْعل، بسّ انا مبحِبِّش اشغّل بالْها لا هِيّ وَلا الوِلاد وَلا احسِّسْهُم بحاجه. مهْما حصل لازِم مَيْشيلوش هُمّا حاجه حتَّى لَوْ انا اللى هسْتحْمِل كُلّ حاجه فى قلْبى و هسْكُت.

مِسِك ابو عمْرو تِليفوْنُه، طلب رقم:

"الو، اُسْتاذ عبْد الكريم. كُنْت عاوْزك تِشوفْلى بيْعه لِشقَّة العُبور..*

"It's nothing."

"Tell me. I'm worried!"

"Argh! Samia! It's nothing, I said."

Om Amr left the room worried and sad. Just like all men, Abu Amr would never say what was bothering him.

Abu Amr thought to himself, "I know that she will feel sad, but I don't like to worry her or the kids or make them feel that there is anything wrong. No matter what has happened, they should never worry about anything, even if that means I keep it all to myself and say nothing."

Abu Amr picked up his phone a dialed a number.

"Hello, Mr. Abd-Alkareem. I wanted you to arrange to sell the El-Oboor apartment."

---

*Many Egyptians own a second apartment in the suburbs as an investment. Here, Abu Amr is calling his real estate agent, having decided to sell his apartment in the suburb of El-Oboor, in order to free up much needed cash.

الفصْل التّامِن: كُبّايِة شاي عنْد الجيران

"يوْم تاني و نفْس **الغُلْب بِتاع كُلّ يوْم..**" فكّرِت أُمّ عمْرو بعْد ما تِعْبِت فى تصْحيّة العِيال، عمايل الفِطار، شيْل مطْرح ما كلوا، غسيل المَواعين، شيْل الغسيل مِن علَى الحبْل، و ترْتيب مطْرح ما كُلّ واحِد رمَى بيجاماتُه.

بصّت أُمّ عمْرو علَى اوْضة عمْرو و ميدو و قالِت: "محدِّش فيهُم حتَّى هايِن عليْه طبْق البطانيه قبْل ما يِنْزِل!"

دخلِت اوْضة هِبه و اِتْضايقِت اكْتر: "حتَّى اِنْتى يا هِبه! **ده انْتى** المفْروض حتَّى بِنْت!"

تِلّ مِن الهِدوم علَى الكراسى و الادْراج مِفتّحه و المكْياج بِتاعْها مِكرْكِب علَى التّسْريحه.

Chapter 8: **Tea at the Neighbors'**

"Another day and the same daily grind," thought Om Amr after she had become tired from waking up the kids, making breakfast, cleaning up after they had eaten, doing the dishes, taking the laundry off the clothesline, and tidying up after everyone has left their pajamas on the floor.

Om Amr looked at Amr and Mido's room and said, "Neither of them even thought of making the bed before leaving."

She went into Heba's room and got more annoyed. "Even you Heba! And you're a girl!"

A pile of clothes on chairs and open drawers and her makeup a mess on the dresser.

الغُلْب بِتاع كُلّ يوْم (lit. *the suffering of every day*)

ده can precede a second-person pronoun to add a tone of belittlement. Notice how the two words are pronounced together: ده اَنْتَ *danta,* ده اَنْتِ *danti,* ده اَنْتوا *dantu.*

"ربِّنا يهُديكى يا بنْتى!" قالتْ أمّ عمْرو فى اِستِسْلام و دخلتِ الحمّام تِتْشطَّف عشان تِلْبِس و تِنْزِل السّوق. لِبْستِ أمّ عمْرو عبايتْها و الطَّرْحه و خدتِ بوك الفِلوس و مفاتيح البيْت و نِزْلِت. دخلتِ السّوق و هتْجيب حاجات بسيطه للغدا، زَىّ اَىّ بيْت مصْرى: بصل و بطاطِس و خِيار و قوطه و فاصولْيا وَلّا كُرُنْبايه...

دخلتِ أمّ عمْرو اوِّل حاجه قابْلتِها بيّاع البصل.

—بكام البصل لَوْ سمحْت؟
—بِتمانْيَه جِنيْه الكيلو.
—تمانْيَه جِنيْه! ليْه؟ ده كان لِسّه بِخمْسه الاِسْبوع اللى فات!
—هُوَّ الدُّنْيا كُلّها بقِت غلا يا سِتّى. لَوْ مِش عاجْبِك شوفى غيْرْنا و هتْلاقى نفس الاسْعار.

مِشْيت أمّ عمْرو مِش مِصدّقه اِزّاى السِّعْر قرّب علىَ الضِّعْف فى اسابيع قُليِّله. كُلّ حاجه فى البلد غِلْيت بعْد زِيادة سِعْر الدّوْلار قُدّام الجِنيْه المصْرى.* بسّ حتَّى الخُضار بيِغْلى ليْه؟ هُوَّ كمان البصل مِسْتَوْرد؟

اِشْترِت أمّ عمْرو الخُضار اللى هِيَّ محْتاجاه و مِشْيت مِش مِصدّقه اِنّها صرفِت ٥٠ جِنيْه علىَ حاجات قُليِّله كِده. ده يادوْب اكْل يومينْ تلاته بسّ.

"God guide you, my daughter!" Om Amr said in despair and and went to the bathroom to wash up and put her clothes on to go to the market. Om Amr put on her abaya and headscarf, took her wallet and the house keys, and went out. She went to the market and just wanted to buy a few things for lunch. Just like any Egyptian home: onion, potatoes, cucumbers, tomatoes, beans, or cabbage....

Om Amr got to the market, and the first thing she saw was the onion vendor.

"How much are the onions, please?"

"Eight pounds a kilo."

"Eight pounds! Why? It was only five last week!"

Everything has gone up, ma'am. If you don't like it, you can go check others and you will find the same prices.

Om Amr walked away, unable to believe how the price had nearly doubled in only a few weeks. Everyrthing in the country had gotten expensive after the devaluation of the Egyptian pound against the dollar. But why have even vegetable prices increased? Are onions also imported?

Om Amr bought the vegetables she needed and walked off, not believing she had spent 50 pounds on just a few things. This is barely a couple of days' food!

*See note on p. 101.

خَمْسِين = ٥٠

vendor in a vegetable market

دخلِت البقاله تِجيب بيْض و لبن و جِبْنه. و ختمِت الجَوْله بِشِرا العيْش فى طابور طَويل قُدَّام المخْبز. النّاس دى كُلّها واقْفه عشان رغيف عيْش عمّال حجْمُه يِصْغر اكْتر و اكْتر معَ الزَّمن.

—صباح الخيْر **يا حاجه** اُمّ عمْرو.
—صباح الخيْر يا عمّ احْمد.
—هاتى عنِّك يا حاجه. بيْشيل مِنْها اِكْياس الطّلبات.
—**كتَّر خيرْك** يا عمّ احْمد. معْلِشّ تاعْبينك معانا.
—لا مفيش تعب ولا حاجه يا سِتّ الكُلّ.

و هِىَّ طالْعه الدّوْر التّالِت لقِت شقّة اُمّ رجاء مفْتوحه.

—اِتْفضّلى يا اُمّ عمْرو! بِتْقولها تِدْخُل تُقْعُد معاها شُوَيّه.
—صباح الخيْر يا اُمّ رجاء... خلاص يا عمّ احْمد حُطّ اِنْتَ الحاجه هِنا. هقْعُد انا شُوَيّه معَ اُمّ رجاء و اطْلع.
—ماشى يا سِتّ هانِم. اَىّ اَوامِر تانْيَه؟
—لا كتّر خيرْك.

She went to the grocer's to buy eggs, milk, and cheese. And she ended her shopping trip with buying bread, [after standing] in a long line in front the baker's. All these people were standing, waiting for a loaf of bread that gets smaller and smaller every time.

"Good morning, Madam Om Amr."

"Good morning, Mr. Ahmed."

"Let me take that from you, Madam," [he said] as he took shopping bags from her.

"Thank you, Mr. Ahmed. I really appreciate all your help."

"No, it's no trouble at all, Ma'am."

While going up to the third floor, she saw the door of Om Ragaa's apartment was open.

"Om Amr, please come in!" asking her in to come in and spend some time with her.

"Good morning, Om Ragaa.... Okay, Mr. Ahmed, you can leave my things here. I'm going to sit with a little with Om Ragaa before I go upstairs."

"Okay, Ma'am. Anything else I can help you with?"

"No, thank you."

يا حاجه (lit. *pilgrim*) is a respectful way to address an elderly woman. Even though Om Amr is only middle-aged, Ahmed uses it to show deference, as he works for her and is of a lower social class.

كتّر خيْرك (lit. *may your bounties increase*) is a way to thank someone sincerely. For more casual, everyday *'thank-you's,* use شُكْراً or مرْسِي (French *merci*).

دخلِت أُمّ عمْرو عنْد أُمّ رجاء الشّقّه.
—لحْسن اكون عطّلْتِك عن حاجه..
—لا وَلا عطله وَلا حاجه. ده انا سِمِعْت خَطَواتِك علىَ السِّلّم افْتكرْتِك أُمّ عبير. دى قايْلالى هتِطْلعْلى مِن ساعه.
—واللهِ! تِلاقيها اِتْشغِلِت فى حاجه وَلّا بِتاع. زمانْها طالْعه...

لِسّه مخلّصِتْش الجُمْله الباب خبط. ضِحْكوا الاتْنيْن و قالوا فى وَقْت واحِد: "الله! دى شكْلها **جت علىَ السّيره**!"

—اِتْفضّلى اِتْفضّلى يا أُمّ عبير. انا و أُمّ عمْرو كُنّا لِسّه بِنْقول رُحْتى فيْن ده كُلُّه.
—سلامو عليْكو، قالِت أُمّ عبير و هِيَّ بِتاخُد نفْسْها.
—و عليْكُم السّلام، اهْلًا و سهْلًا يا أُمّ عبير. بقالى كِتير مشُفْتِكيش، أُمّ عمْرو قالِت.
—اه والله مشْغوله جِدّاً فى **جهاز** البِتّ عبير.
—ما شاء الله ما شاء الله، ربِّنا يِتمِّمْلها بِخيْر، قالِت أُمّ عمْرو.
—ربِّنا يِخلّيكى، و **عُقْبال** هِبه و كُلّ البنات.
—امين يا ربّ ، أُمّ عمْرو و أُمّ رجاء فى نفس واحِد.

Om Amr went into Om Ragaa's [apartment].

"I hope I'm not keeping you from anything."

"No, not at all. I heard your steps on the stairs and thought you were Om Abeer. She told me she was coming up to visit an hour ago."

"Oh, really? Maybe she got busy doing stuff. She'll be here soon…"

She hadn't quite finished her sentence when there was a knock at the door. The two laughed and said at the same time, "Oh! Speak of the devil!"

"Come in, come in, Om Ameer. Om Amr and I were just wondering where you've been all this time."

"As-salaamu alaykum!" Om Abeer said, catching her breath.

"Wa alaykum assalaam. Welcome, Om Abeer. Long time no see," said Om Amr.

"Yes, you're right. I've been really busy buying things for when my daughter Abeer gets married."

"Oh, that's so great! God bless her," said Om Amr.

"Thank you. Heba is next, God willing, and all girls."

"Amen," said Om Amr and Om Ragaa in unison.

جه على السّيره (lit. *to come at the mention*) is used when someone appears just after being mentioned in conversation.

جهاز – See p. 121.

عُقْبال is used to wish single people marriage. For example, when a single person congratulates newlyweds, their response would be عُقْبالك, the sentiment being *And I hope the same for you (someday)*.

قامِت اُمّ رجاء تِعمِلُهُم شاي و قدّمتلُهُم موز و بُرتُقان.
—مِنوّرين والله.
—بِنورِك يا اُمّ رجاء، تِعِبتى نفْسِك ليْه؟
—لا وَلا تعب وَلا حاجه.
اُمّ عبير بدأِت الكلام: "ده احْنا عشان نِجيب **جِهاز البِتّ** عبير ابوها دفع اللى وَراه و اللى قُدّامُه. ايْه اللى حصل فى الاسْعار ده!"
—اه والله، ردِّت اُمّ عمرو و اُمّ رجاء.
—ده مِش بسّ فى الاجْهِزه الكهْربائيْه اللى بقِت بدل الخمسْتلاف عشره، لا كمان فى المفْروشات و السّتايِر و السّجاجيد. وَلّا حاجات الطّبْخ بقَى!
—**لا حَوْلَ وَلا قُوَّه اِلّا بِالله!**
—نصيحه والله، اِلْحقوا جيبوا لِبناتْكو جِهازْهُم قبْل ما الحاجه تِغْلَى اكْتر مِن كِده!
ردِّت اُمّ عمْرو: "و هُوَّ حدّ بقَى معاه حاجه؟ الحال واقِف و ماشْيَه بِالسِّتْر. ده حتَّى اللَّحْمه و الفِراخ النّاس مبقِتْش عارْفه تِجيبْهُم مرّه فى الشَّهْر حتَّى!"

Om Ragaa got up to go make them tea and served them bananas and oranges.

"Here you are."

"Thank you, Om Ragaa. You didn't have to go to so much trouble."

"No trouble at all."

Om Abeer began talking, "In order to buy things for Abeer getting married, her father had to spend everything we had. What's going on with prices!"

"Yes, you're right," Om Amr and Om Ragaa replied.

"It's not only electronics which, instead of five thousand, now cost ten, but also, furniture, curtains, carpets… and don't get me started with kitchenware!"

"Oh, dear God!"

"Some advice: hurry up and buy things for your daughter's new household before prices go up more."

Om Amr replied, "But does anyone have money? Times are tough. Even meat and chicken, people can no longer afford to eat but once a month!"

مِنوّرين (m. مِنوّر; f. مِنوّره) literally means *You are illuminating (my home)*. The reply is بنورك (f. بِنورِك; pl. بِنورْكو): *With your light!* or مِنوّر باهْلُه *It is illuminated by its family.*

جهاز – preparations for a daughter's marriage, especially buying furniture and other things for her new house.

البِتّ – Mothers often precede their son's or daughter's name by الواد and البِتّ, respectively, when talking to others about them, especially when complaining.

لا حَوْلَ وَلا قُوّه إلّا بالله – See note on p. 107.

—اه والله، ردّت أُمّ رجاء، و كُلّ جزّار ليه تسعيره! **تِقولْش** بورْصه؟

—لا و لمّا تِسْأليهُم ليْه الاسْعار بِتِغْلَى يِقولّك اصل العلْف مِسْتوْرد! طب ما تأكّلوهُم فول وَلَّا دُره! اذا كان **البنى ادْمين** بِياكُلوا فول كُلّ يوْم، البهايِم بِقِت احْسن مِنِّنا!

—والله عنْدِك حقّ يا أُمّ رجاء، ردّت أُمّ عبير.

واجْهِت أُمّ عبير الكلام لِأُمّ عمْرو: "و اِنْتِك عمْرو عامِل ايه فى الدِّراسه؟ السّنه دى ثانويه عامّه بقَى!"

—والله **مِطلَّع عيْنى** انا و ابوه! علَى قلْبُه مراوِح! وَلَا كاِنُّه ثناويه عامّه وَلَا زِفْت. تاعِبْنا فى الصَّحيان و المُذاكْره و علَى طول بِيرْجع مِتْأخَّر.

—هُمّا كُلُّهُم كِده والله تعب! حتَّى الواد عبْدُ الرَّحْمن اِبْنى. المفْعوص لِسَّه فى اِعْدادى و تاعِبْنا برْضُه، ردّت أُمّ رجاء.

—صُحابْهُم فى المدارِس هُمّا السّبب. بِيِتْلمّوا علَى بعْض و كُلّ واحِد فيهُم بِيْبوّظ التّانى، قالِت أُمّ عبير.

—فِعْلاً بِجدّ! **الواحِد** بِيْبقَى تعْبان فى ترْبِيِّتْهُم و يِيجى صُحابْهُم يِبوّظوهُم! قالِت أُمّ عمْرو فى حسْره.

بعْد ما الكلام بقَى تِقيل، أُمّ رجاء قالِت تِلطّف الجَوّ و تِفْتح موْضوع اخفّ.

"You're right," agreed Om Ragaa. "and every butcher sets his own price as if it were the stock market!"

"And when you ask them why the prices are going up, they say it's because animal fodder is imported! Then feed them beans or corn! Human beings eat beans every day. Are livestock better than us now?"

"Yes. You're right, Om Ragaa," replied Om Abeer.

Om Abeer addressed Om Amr, "And how is your son Amr at school? This is his senior year of high school!"

"He is driving me and his father insane. He's so laid back! Not like he's a high school senior or anything. We're exhausted having to wake him up, make him study, and he's always late."

"They're all like that, a pain in the butt. Even my son, Abdelrahman. The little bastard is still in middle school and is already giving us a hard time," Om Ragaa replied.

"Their friends from school are the reason. They bond and ruin each other," Om Abeer said.

"So true! You put so much effort and time into raising them, then their friends come along and ruin them!" Om Amr said in despair.

After the conversation had gotten a bit heavy, Om Ragaa thought to change the subject to something lighter.

تِقولْش – Notice 1) The masculine singular اِنْتَ verb form is used impersonally.

2) The negative suffix ش is used here without م in a rhetorical question.

بنى ادم (lit. *son of Adam;* f. بِنى ادْمه; pl. بِنى ادْمين) *human being*

مطلّع عينى (lit. *pulling out my eye*) *making me pull my hair out; driving me crazy*

الواحِد is an impersonal pronoun, like *one* or *you* in English.

—إلّا صحيح يا أمّ عبير، كُنتى قُلْتيلى هتْقوليلى علىَ وَصْفة البَطاطِس بالكُفْته الجِديده دى.

—والله؟ وَصْفة ايْه دى يا أمّ عبير؟ سألِت أمّ عمرو فى فُضول.

—دى وَصْفه كِده البِتّ عبير جابِتها مِن النّت بما اِنّها بِتِتعلِّم فينا قبْل الجَواز.

—ها ها ها، اه خلّيها تِتْعلِّم فيكو بدل ما تِتْعلِّم فى جوزْها! قالت أمّ رجاء.

—المُهمّ ايْه بقَى: بِتْجيبى بصلايَه، تِقْطعيها شرايح و تِفْرشى بيها الصَّينيه بعْد ما تحُطِّى نُقْطِة زيت. بعْديْن تِقْطعى بطاطِسْتيْن شرايح و تحُطّيها فوْق البصل، بعْديْن شرايح طماطِم. بعْديْن تيجى بقَى للّحْمه المفْرومه و تحُطّى عليها مِلْح و فِلْفِل و كُزْبره. و تِكوّريها و تحُطّيها علىَ وشّ الصّينيه. بعْديْن تِصبّى شُويَّة مرقه بسّ مِش كِتير عشان البصله و الطماطِم هتْنزِّل ميّتْها بعْديْن.

—الله! دى وَصْفه سهْله و جميله خالِص! قالت أمّ عمرو.

—اه و لَوْ عنْدِك فِلْفِل حُطّى عليْها هتِطْلع تُحْفه معاكى! كمِّلت أمّ عبير.

—و تِتّاكِل بقَى بِرُزّ وَلّا عيْش؟ سألِت أمّ رجاء.

—واللهِ اللى تِحِبّيه! بسّ معَ الرُزّ مُمْتازه و هتْشبَّع، أمّ عبير ردّت.

"Oh, by the way, Om Abeer, you told me you would give me that new recipe for potatoes with meatballs."

"Oh really? What recipe, Om Abeer?" asked Om Amr with curiosity.

"It's a recipe that Abeer found on the Internet as she is trying things out on us before she gets married."

"Ha, ha, ha! Yes, let her learn on you instead of trying it out on her husband," Om Ragaa said.

"So anyway, here's the recipe: You take an onion, cut it into slices, and cover the tray with it after putting a little oil on it. Then you slice up one potato and put it on top of the onion, then tomato slices. Then you take minced meat, salt and pepper it, and add coriander. Make it into balls and put them on the surface of the tray. Finally, you pour on some broth, but not too much because the onion and tomato will produce juices later.

"Wow! That's an easy recipe and [it sounds] delicious!" said Om Amr.

"Oh, and if you have green peppers, add them to it. It'll be fantastic!" Om Abeer continued.

"And is it served with rice or bread?" Om Ragaa asked.

"Well, whichever you prefer, but with rice, it's great and will fill you up," Om Abeer replied.

إلّا can come at the beginning of an utterance to express that you just remembered to mention something: إلّا كُنْت عايِز اسْألك *Oh, tell me...*؛ إلّا قولّ *Oh, I wanted to ask you...*

—جَزاكى الله كُلّ خيْر، قالِت اُمّ رجاء.
—انا هقوم **انا اتْوكّل علَى الله**، لحْسن ميدو **زمانُه هَيرْجع** مِن المدْرسه. الْحق اعْملُه الغدا! قالِت اُمّ عمْرو.
—ماشى اِتْفضّلى، قالِت اُمّ رجاء.
—سلامو عليْكو.
—و عليْكُم السّلام. متْغيبيش بقَى عليْنا يا اُمّ عمْرو. خلّينا نِشوفِك! قالِت اُمّ عبير.
—حاضِر ماشى. معَ السّلامه.

طِلْعِت اُمّ عمْرو شقِّتْها و دخلِت البيْت الفاضى و قالِت فى نفْسها:
"رِجِعْنا تانى لِلغُلْب.."

"Thank you so much," Om Ragaa said.

"I'll take off now. Mido's coming home soon, and I should start making him lunch!" Om Amr said.

"Okay, let me show you out," Om Ragaa said.

"Bye!"

"Good-bye. Don't be a stranger, Om Amr! See you again soon!" Om Abeer said.

"All right, sure! Bye!"

Om Amr went up to her apartment and into the empty house and said to herself, "Back to the grind!"

جزاك الله كُلّ خيْر (also: الله يجزيك خير; lit. *May God reward you!*) is an expression of gratitude: *Thanks!*

انا اتْوكِّل علىَ الله (lit. *I'll put my trust in God.*) is used to signal one is departing. (See also note on p. 105.)

زمانهُ *at any moment; by now* (in other words, *at the expected time*)

الفصْل التّاسِع: محفْظِة الاحْلام

ميدو خرج مِن المدْرسه و كان ماشى فى اِتِّجاه مَوْقِف الميكروباصات لمّا سِمِع صاحْبُه عُمر بيْناديه.

—يا ميدو اِسْتنّانى همْشى معاك.
—اِنْتَ طريقك مِش كان النّاحْيَه التّانْيَه؟
—لا ما انا النّهارْده هروح عنْد خالْتى اللى فى شُبْرا.
—اه كُوَيِّس، هتْوَنِّسْنى فى الطّريق يَعْنى.

مِشى عُمر و ميدو و بعْديْن ميدو داس علَى حاجه طريه فا بيْبُصّ تحْتُه يِشوف هُوَّ داس علَى ايْه. طِلْعِت محْفظه جِلْد مليْانه فلوس.

—بُصّ يا عُمر لقيْت ايْه!
—يا نهار ابْيَض ده شكْلها فِلوس كِتيره اوى!

Chapter 9: **The Wallet of Dreams**

Mido left school and was walking to the bus station when he heard his friend Omar calling him.

"Mido, wait for me! I'm coming with you!"

"Don't you go the other way?"

"No, today I'm going to visit my aunt who lives in Shoubra."

"Oh, good. I'll have company then."

Mido and Omar started walking. Then Mido stepped on something soft so he looked down to see what it was. It turned out to be a leather wallet full of money.

"Omar, look what I found!"

"Oh my God! That looks like a lot of money."

ميدو مَيعْرفْش كُلّ اَوْراق الفلوس بسّ هُوَّ اكْبَر وَرقه عارفْها كانِت العِشْرين جنِيه* اللى مامْتُه بِتْدّيهالُه لَوْ هَيِشْترى حاجه من البقاله. و دايْماً تِقولُّه خُد بالك اوِعَى تِنْسَى تاخُد الباقى وَلَّا تِوَقَّعُه. لكن جُوَّه المحْفظه دى اَوْراق كتِيره عِشْرين و اوْراق تانْيَه مامْتُه مش بِترْضى تِدّيهالُه لحْسن تِضِيع.

—يا بخْتك يا صاحْبى! هتِعْمِل ايْه بِكُلّ الفلوس دى!

ميدو بصّلُه و هُوَّ مِش مِسْتَوْعِب فِكْرِة انُّه ياخُد الفلوس دى كُلّها. رِجِع عُمَر يِكَمِّل:
—انْتَ مُمْكِن تِشْترى حَلَوِيّات كتِيره! عارِف الشُّكولاته الكبِيره اللى بِالبُنْدُق اللى عُمَر ما مصروفْنا كفَّى نِجِيبْها؟ دِلْوَقْتى مُمْكِن نِجيب مِنْها كتِير!

ميدو بدأ يِحِسّ بِالحماسه و قال: "اَيْوَه اَيْوَه و نِدْخُل ماكْدونالْدْز نِجِيب خمْسه هابى ميل!"
—وَلَّا محلّات اللِّعب! مُمْكِن نِجيب عربِيه بِرِيموْت كونْتْروْل و طيّاره هِلِيكوبْتر و سْبايْدِر مان!

ميدو عيْنُه لمعِت اوى و قال لعُمَر: "طيِّب يَلَّا بِينا! فيه محلّ كبِير بتاع لعِب قُريّب مِن هِنا." جِرى ميدو و عُمَر و وصْلوا المحلّ. وقْفوا قُدّام الفِترِينه و شاف السْكوتر الازْرق اللى بِيِلْمع و لِيه كشّاف مِن قُدّام. ميدو فِضِل يحْلم انُّه يِشْتِريه و ياخْدوا بِيه يِلْعب على سُطوح العِماره بِتاعِتْهُم.

Mido didn't know all the bills. The biggest one he knew was the 20-pound bill, which his mom would give him when he bought something from the grocer's. She would keep telling him to be careful and not to forget to get change or lose it. However, inside this wallet, there were a lot of 20s and other bills that his mom wouldn't give him, afraid he'd lose them.

"You're so lucky, my friend! What are you going to do with all that money?"

Mido looked at him, unable to believe the idea of taking all this money. Omar resumed,

"You can buy lots of sweets! You know that large chocolate with nuts that our pocket money is never enough to buy? Now we can buy a lot of it!"

Mido started to feel excited and said, "Yes, yes! And go to McDonald's and buy five Happy Meals!"

"Or toy stores! We can buy a car with a remote control and a helicopter and a Spider-Man!"

Mido's eyes glowed and he said to Omar, "Okay, let's go! There's a big toy store near here." Mido and Omar ran and arrived at the shop. They stood in front of the shop window and he saw a shiny blue scooter with a headlight. Mido kept dreaming that he bought it and took it to play with on the roof of their building.

---

*Egyptian banknotes in circulation are: 25 and 50 piastres; 1, 5, 10, 20, 50, 100, and 200-pound bills.

—ميدو وَله يا ميدو!
صوْت عُمر صاحْبُه فوّقُه مِن الحِلْم.
—ايْه؟
—شايِف الطيّاره الهِليكوبْتر دى!
—الله! حِلْوَه اوى!
—مكْتوب عليْها ب ٤٥٠ جِنيْه. تِفْتِكِر اِحْنا معانا كام؟
—مِش عارِف!

دخلوا شارِع جانِبى صُغيّر و طلّعوا المحْفظه. و بصّ ميدو علىَ الارْقام المكْتوبه علىَ الفِلوس عشان يِعِدّوه.

—٢٠٠ زايِد ١٠٠ زايِد ٢٠٠.. مِش عارِف ده كِتير. اِجْمع اِنْتَ كِده!

ميدو طلّع الاله الحاسْبه مِن شنطِتُه و حسب. طِلع ١٥٠٠.

—دول ١٥٠٠!
—يالهْوى! ده احْنا مُمْكِن نِجيب طيّارْتيْن مِن دول! واحْده ليّا و واحْده ليك!

"Mido! Hey, Mido!" His friend Omar's voice brought him back from his dreams.

"What?"

"Do you see this helicopter?"

"Oh my God! It's so nice!"

"It has 450 pounds written on it. How much do you think we have?"

"I don't know!"

They went down a small side street and took out the wallet. Mido looked at the numbers written on the bills to count them.

"200 plus 100 plus 200... I don't know. It's a lot. You count."

Mido took the calculator out of his bag and started counting. It turned out to be 1,500.

"It's 1,500!"

"Oh boy! We could buy two of these helicopters! One for me and one for you!"

رُبْعُميه و خَمْسين = ٤٥٠

ميه = ١٠٠; ميتينْ = ٢٠٠

ألْف و خُمْسُميه = ١٥٠٠

يالهْوى *Oh my God!* (expression of dismay)

بصّ ميدو لِلفلوس و بعْديْن و هُوَّ بيقْفِل المحْفظه شاف فى الجيْب التّانى صورةِ الرّاجِل معاه بِنْتُه الصُّغيّره و اِبْنُه. فِضِل ميدو باصِص لِلصّوره و باين علَى وشُّه الحُزْن. عُمر صاحْبُه بصَّلُه و سأله:

— مالك يا ميدو؟

— بُصّ يا عُمر.. وَراه صورةِ الابّ و اَوْلادُه.

قال ميدو: "دِلْوَقْتى انا لَوْ جِبْت بِالفلوس دى طيّاره و كُلّ حاجه نِفْسى فيها، مُمْكِن الابّ المِسْكين ده مَيعْرفْش يجيب لِبِنْتُه الصُّغيّره دى هِدوم العيد، اَوْ يجيب لِاِبْنُه الصُّغيّر ده كيس شيبْسى. يِمْكِن..يِمْكِن حتَّى مَيعْرفوش يجيبوا اكْل!"

كُلّ ما فكّر ميدو زِعِل مِن نفْسُه و خاف اكْتر و اكْتر.

— بسّ هُوَّ راجِل كِبير هَيِعْرف يِتْصرّف لكِن انا و اِنْتَ مِش هنِعْرف نِجيب فِلوس زَىّ دى تانى.

بصّ ميدو لِعُمر و رِجِع يبُصّ لِلصّوره و هُوَّ مِحْتار يِعْمِل ايه و يِرْجع يبُصّ لِلسُّكوتر و الطيّاره و ادّ ايه هُوَّ نفْسُه فيهُم.

— يِمْكِن الفِلوس دى ظهرِت قُدّامْنا عشان ربّنا عارِف اِنّنا هنِفْرح بيها! زَىّ الهِديه مثلاً، عُمر قال.

Mido looked at the money. And then, as he was closing the wallet, he saw, in another compartment, a photo of the man and his little daughter and son. Mido kept looking at the photo, and an expression of sadness came over his face. Omar looked at him and asked,

"What's wrong, Mido?"

"Look, Omar!" He showed him the photo of the father and his kids.

Mido said, "If I use this money now to buy the helicopter and everything I want, this poor father might not be able to buy holiday clothes for his little girl or a bag of chips for his little son. They might... might not even be able to buy food!"

The more Mido thought, the sadder he made himself feel, and the more and more scared he got.

"But he's a grown-up man he'll figure out what to do. But you and I will never get the chance to have money like this again."

Mido looked at Omar then looked back at the photo, torn between what to do. Then he looked back at the scooter and the helicopter, thinking how much he wanted to have them.

"Maybe this money appeared before us because God knows how happy we will be with it! Like a gift or something!" Omar said.

فكّر ميدو فى كلام عُمر. هل مُمْكِن فِعْلاً يكون ربِّنا اللى بعتْلُهُم الهِديه دى؟ لكِن ربِّنا برْضُه قال اِنَّنا لازِم نِكون عِنْدِنا امانه و مِنسْرقْش حاجة الغيّر. مامْتُه دايْماً علّمِتُه كِده. كمان اِفْرض النَّاس دى مبقِتْش عارفه تلاقى فِلوس للاكْل و اللِّبْس، ربِّنا اكيد هَيِزْعل مِنُّه.

—يا ميدو، ساكِت ليْه؟ ناداه عُمر.
—لا يا عُمر. انا لا يِمْكِن اعْمِل حاجه زَيّ كِده! انا لازِم ارجّع للرّاجِل ده محْفظْتُه و فِلوسُه.
—بسّ يا ميدو..!
—لا متْقولْش حاجه. انا لازِم اعْمِل كِده. انا لَوْ ضاعِت مِنّى حاجه هحِبّ لَوْ النَّاس اللى لقِتْها رجّعِتْهالى. زمانُه دِلْوَقْتى بِيْدوّر عليْها و قلْقان.
—طب اِحْنا هنِعْرف نِوْصلُه اِزّاى؟

سِكِت ميدو و فكّر كِده. اِزّاى فِعْلاً هَيْلاقى الرّاجِل ده؟

—مِش عارِف..

فجْأه جه لِميدو فِكْره. و بدأ يِدوّر فى جيوب المحْفظه التّانْيه لحدّ ما لقَى كارْت الشّخْص و مكْتوب عليْه اِسْمُه و رقمُه.

Mido thought about what Omar said. Could God really be the one who sent them this gift? But doesn't God also say that we should be honest and never steal others' stuff? His mom always teaches him that. Also, what if these people couldn't find money for food and clothes. God would definitely be mad at him.

"Mido, why you are not saying anything?" Omar called out.

"No, Omar. I can't do that! I must give that man his wallet and money."

"But Mido..!"

"No, don't say anything. I must do it. If it was me who lost something, I would like the people who found it to return it to me. He must be looking for it now, worried."

"Okay, but how are we going find him?"

Mido was silent for a moment and thought. Yes, how is he going to find that man?

"I don't know."

Suddenly, Mido got an idea. He started looking through the wallet's other compartments until he found the man's business card with his name and number on it.

اِفْرِض (lit. *Suppose...*) *What if...?*

—لقيْتُه! بابا دايماً بيْحُطّ كُروت زَيّ دى فى مَحْفَظْتُه فيها اِسْم و عُنْوان الصَّيْدليه. يَلّا بينا يا عُمر نروح اَىّ كُشْك نِتِّصل بيه.

راح عُمر و ميدو لاِقْرب كُشْك لقوه و طلبوا رقم الرّاجل:

—الو؟

—اَيْوَه، قال ميدو بِصوْت مِترْعِش.

—**اَيْوَه مين معايا؟**

—حضْرتك اُسْتاذ عادِل؟

—اَيْوَه، مين؟

—انا لقيْت مَحْفظة حضْرتك..

—يا نهار ابْيَض! ده انا حتَّى مخدْتِش بالى اِنّها وقِعت مِنّى غيْر دِلْوَقْتى لمّا قُلْتِلى! شُكْراً يا اِبْنى اِنْتَ فيْن و هاجيلك.

—عنْد شارِع مُصدَّق قُدّام محلّ Top Toys.

—ماشى دقايِق و هكون عنْدك.

وقِف ميدو و عُمر شُوَيّه و بعْديْن لقوا راجل نِزِل مِن عربيه سوْدا كِبيره و بيِتْلِفِّت حَواليْه. قرّب مِنْهُم الرّاجل و سأل: "حدّ فيكو اِسْمُه ميدو؟"

—اَيْوَه انا. حضْرتك اُسْتاذ عادِل؟

—مظْبوط.

—اِتفضّل.

"I found it! Dad always keeps one of these business cards in his wallet with the number and address of the pharmacy. Let's go to a telephone booth we can call him from."

Omar and Mido went to the nearest booth they could find and called the man.

"Hello?"

"Hello," Mido said in a quivering voice.

"Yes, who's calling?"

"Are you Mr. Adel?"

"Yes, who is this?"

"I found your wallet..."

"Oh God! I didn't even notice that I lost it until you told me now! Thank you, young man! Tell me where you are and I will come to you."

"On Mosaddak Street, in the front of Top Toys toy store."

"Okay. I'll be there in a few minutes."

Mido and Omar were there for a while. Then they saw a man getting out of a big black car and looking around. The man approached and asked them, "Is one of you named Mido?"

"Yes, I am. Are you Mr. Adel?"

"That's right."

"Here you are."

مين معايا (lit. *Who is with me?*) is used on the telephone to ask who is calling. You wil often hear talk show hosts say مين معانا؟ when taking calls from viewers.

ميدو ادّاله المحفظه و الرّاجل شكرُه و عدّ الفلوس. لقاه منقِصتْش وَلَّا مِلّيم و اِسْتغرب جدّاً. هُوَّ كان فاكر عشان قالوله يِيجى قُدّام محلّ الالْعاب انّهُم خدوا مِن الفلوس و اِشْتروا لعْبه وَلَّا حاجه.

—مُمْكن اسألك ليه مخدّوش حتّى شُوَيّه مِن الفلوس تِشْتِروا اَىّ حاجه؟

ميدو بصّ باحْراج و تَوَتُّر و قال: "اااا..عشان دى فِلوس حضْرتك و مُمْكن تِكون مِحْتاجْها عشان بِنْتك و اِنْك.

—بِنْتى و اِنى! و اِنْتَ عِرِفْت ازّاى؟

ردّ عُمر: "ما احْنا شُفْنا الصّوره اللى فى المحفظه.

—اَيْوَه صحيح! بسّ اِنْتَ شاطِر اوى يا ميدو اِنَّك لقيْت الكارْت و اتِّصلْت بِيَّا. شُكراً جِدّاً ليك يا ميدو.

—العفْو.

و عادِل جاىّ يِمْشى سِمِع عُمر بِيْقول لِشادى.

—شُفْت؟ طِلِع غنّى اهو و عنْدُه عربيه كبيره! يَعْنى لَوْ كُنّا خدْنا الفِلوس جِبْنا بيها اللُّعْبه مكانْش هَيحْصل حاجه وَلَّا مِش هَيْلاقوا ياكْلوا وَلَّا اَىّ حاجه.

ضِحِك عادِل و لفّ و قال:
—ميدو..
—اَيْوَه؟

Mido gave him the wallet. The man thanked him and counted the money. He found that not even a penny was missing, and he was shocked. He thought when they told him that they were in front of a toy store that they would have taken some money and bought a toy or something.

"Can I ask why you didn't take even a little money and buy anything?"

Mido looked embarrassed and nervous and said, "Ah... because it's your money, sir. And you might need it for you daughter and son."

"My daughter and son! How do you know?"

Omar replied, "We saw the picture of them in the wallet."

"Yes, of course! But you are so smart Mido for finding my business card and calling me. Thank you so much, Mido."

"You're welcome."

As Adel was leaving, he heard Omar saying to Mido,

"You see! He's a rich man and has a fancy car! So, if we had taken the money, nothing would have happened, like they wouldn't be able to eat or any of that."

Adel smiled, turned to them, and said:

"Mido..."

"Yes?"

—انا كُنْت حابِب اشْكُرك علىَ امانْتك و مُكافْأه ليك انا عاوِز اشْتِريلك هِديه مِن المحلّ ده.
بصّ مِيدو لِمحلّ الالْعاب و هُوَّ مِش مِصدّق و قال بِكْسوف:
—لا مفيش داعى حضْرِتك.
—لا لا انا مُصِرّ.
—يَلّا يا مِيدو متبْقاش رِخِم!
دخل مِيدو و عُمر و أُسْتاذ عادِل المحلّ و قال لِمِيدو اِخْتار اللى اِنْتَ عاوْزُه و مَيْهِمّكْش. مِيدو راح خد سْبايْدر مان صُغيّر و رِجِع قال: "ده عاجِبْنى."
—بسّ ده؟! ده صُغيّر خالِص. اِخْتار حاجه كِبيره شُوَيّه، قال عادِل.
—ايْوَه يا مِيدو قولُّه علىَ الطّ..
—لا لا هُوَّ ده اللى انا عاوْزُه، ردّ مِيدو بِسُرْعه و سكِّت عُمْر.
—ماشى يا سيدى زَىّ ما تِحِبّ!

دفع عادِل فِلوس سْبايْدر مان و رِكِب عربيتُه و مِشى. بعْد ما مِشى قال عُمر:
—ليه يا مِيدو مجِبْتِش الطّياره؟
—لِانّها غالْيَه جِدّاً و انا معمِلْتِش كِده عشان اخُد حاجه فى المُقابِل و اِنْتَ عارِف ده.
—ايْوَه بسّ دى كانِت فُرْصه كُوَيّسه جِدّاً!
—يَلّا نِرْكب و نِروح البيْت هنِتْأخّر!

"I wanted to thank you for your honesty. And as a thank-you gift, I would like to buy you something from this store."

Mido looked at the toy store, unable to believe it and said, embarrassed,

"No, there's no need for that, sir."

"No, no. I insist."

"Come on, Mido. Don't be stubborn," Omar said.

"Mido, Omar, and Mr. Adel went in the store. Adel said to Mido, "Pick anything you want and don't worry about anything. Mido went and got a little Spider-Man toy and said, "I like this one."

"That's all? It's so small. Pick something a bit bigger," Adel said.

"Yes, Mido. Ask him for the heli..."

"No, no! This is what I want," Mido replied quickly to silence Omar.

"Okay, buddy. Whatever you want!"

Adel paid for the Spider-Man, got in his car, and left. After he had left, Omar asked,

"Why didn't you buy the helicopter, Mido?"

"Because it's so expensive, and I didn't do [what I did] to get something in return. You know that."

"Yes, but it was a great opportunity!"

"Let's get the bus and go home. We're going to be late."

وِصِل ميدو البيْت و مامْتُه فتحِتْلُه الباب و لقِت فى إيدُه سبايدر مان و سألتُه:

—جِبْتُه مِنيْن ده يا حبيبى؟
—ده هِديه.
—هِديه؟
—اه هِديه عشان كُنْت النّهارْده كُوِّيِّس..

Mido got home and his mom opened the door for him. She saw the Spider-Man toy in his hand and asked,

"Where did you get that from, honey?"

"It's a gift."

"A gift?"

"Yes. A gift for being a good boy today."

الفصْل العاشِر: مخْطوف

خرج ميدو مِن المدْرسه و راح وقِف يِسْتنَّى **ميكْروباص رمْسيس** كالعاده. فِضِل واقِف وَقْت طَويل و مفيش حاجه راضْيَه تيجى. و كُلّ ما ييجى واحِد يِطْلع ملْيان يا يِتْملى قبْل ما ميدو يِلْحق يِرْكب.

"الجَوّ حرّ اوى. مِش قادِر. بقالى كِتير واقِف و كُلّ ما ميكْروباص رمْسيس ييجى ملْحقْش ارْكب. تعِبْت اوى."

كُلّ ده كان بِيْدور فى تفْكير ميدو و هُوّ واقِف فى الشّمْس شايِل شنْطِتُه التّقيله. مرّه واحْده ميكْروباص اِسْود جه وقِف قُدّامُه و اوِّل ما الباب اِتْفتح جه هَوا ساقِع مِن جوّه مِن التّكْييف.

"الله! ميكْروباص بِتكْييف و فاضى!" فكّر ميدو و جِرى بِسُرْعه.

Chapter 10: **Kidnapped**

Mido left school and went to wait for the Ramses microbus, as usual. He waited and waited for a long time, but nothing came. And whenever one came, it was either full or would fill up before he could get in.

"It's too hot. I can't [stand it anymore]. I've been standing here for so long, and every time a Ramses microbus comes, I can't get in. I'm so tired."

All this was going on in Mido's head while he was standing in the sun carrying his heavy bag. Suddenly, a black microbus stopped in front of him. And as soon as the door opened, cold air came from the air-conditioning inside.

"Wow! A microbus with air-conditioning, and it's empty!" Mido thought and ran quickly.

microbuses at Ramses Station

—لَوْ سمحْت، لَوْ سمحْت. بتْروح رمْسيس؟
بصّ الرَّاجِل لِميدو و بعْدين بصّ حَواليْه و بعْديْن قالُه: "اه يا حبيبى، بسّ متِقولْش بقَى بِصوْت عالى عشان النَّاس متِجْريش عليْك و تاخُد الاماكِن كُلّها. يَلَّا اِطْلع."
—طيِّب..الاُجْره بِكام؟
—بِجِنيْه عادى يا حبيبى. متْخافْش.
—بِجدّ؟ الله!

اِتْبسط ميدو اِنّ الميكْروباص المُكيَّف و الفاضى ده بِجْنيْه بسّ. و بعْد ما قعد لقَى الرَّاجِل بيِقْفِل الباب و بيِقول لِلسَّوَّاق: "اِطْلع يا اسْطَى!"

ميدو اِتْخضّ و قال بخوْف: "يِطْلع فيْن! كُلّ النَّاس دى عاوْزه رمْسيس. ليْه محدِّش غيْرى رِكِب!"

لمّا حسّ الرَّاجِل اِنّ ميدو هَيِبْدأ يِعْمِل دوْشه قالُه: "اَيْوَه اَيْوَه طبعاً اِحْنا بسّ هنِرْكن قُدَّام شُويَّه عشان فيه عربيه قافْلين عليْها."

اِتَّصل الرَّاجِل بِحدّ علَى التِّليفوْن و اِتْكلِّم بِصوْت واطى و ميدو مكانْش سامع بِيْقول ايه. شُويَّه و طِلع جُوَّه الميكْروباص سِتّ.

—سلامو عليْكو. مُمْكِن اقْعُد جنْبك يا حبيبى؟
—اِتْفضَّلى.
—انا هنْزِل رمْسيس. و اِنْتَ؟

"Excuse me, excuse me. Are you going to Ramses?"

The man looked at Mido and then looked around. Then he said, "Yes, sweetie. But don't say that too loud or people will run and take all the seats. Come on, get in."

"All right. How much is the fare?"

"One pound, as usual. Don't worry."

"Oh, really? Cool!"

Mido was happy that this air-conditioned, empty microbus was only one pound. After he sat down, he saw the man close the door and say to the driver, "Go!"

Mido panicked and said, scared, "Go where?! All these people want a Ramses [bus]. Why didn't anyone else get in?"

When the man felt that Mido would start making trouble, he said to him, "Yes, yes, of course! We'll just stop a little further ahead because we were blocking a car."

The man called someone on the phone and talked in a low voice. Mido couldn't hear what he was saying. A few moments later, a woman got in the microbus.

"As-salamu alaykum. Can I sit next to you, honey?"

"Go ahead."

"I'm getting out at Ramses. What about you?"

بِارْتِياح قال ميدو: "اَيْوَه و انا كمان! هُوَّ ليْه محدِّش تانى طِلِع؟"

—ااا..اصْلُه لِسَّه جاىّ قبْل ده علىَ طول ميكْروباص تانى و رِكِب كُلّ اللى علىَ المحطّه. لكِن انا و اِنْتَ حظّنا حِلْو و لقِيْنا ميكْروباص فاضى و فيه تكْيِيف و ستايِر.

—اَيْوَه.

ريَّح ميدو راسُه علىَ ضهْر الكنبه و راح فى النوْمِ. لمّا صحِى لقَى نفْسُه نايِم فى مكان مَيِعْرفوش. اِتْخضّ ميدو و قام يِجْرى يِدوّر علىَ باب. شدَّ الباب بسّ مبْيِفْتحْش. ميدو عيْنُه دمّعِت مِن الخوْف و بعْدِين سِمِع صوْت مِن برّه الباب. جاب ميدو كُرْسى و بصّ مِن فتْحِة مِفْتاح الباب. شاف السِّتّ اللى كانِت فى الميكْروباص هِىّ و السَّوّاق و الرّاجِل اللى كان علىَ الباب. الكُرْسى اللى كان واقِف عليْه ميدو اِتْهزّ و كان هَيْقع.

—سِمِعْتوا الصّوْت ده؟ قال السَّوّاق.
—لا فيه حاجه وَلّا ايْه؟ ردّ الرّاجِل التّانى.
—يِمْكِن الواد صِحِى، ردِّت السِّتّ.
—لمّا اروح اشوف فيه ايْه، قال الرّاجِل.

Relaxed, Mido said, "Yes, me, too! Why didn't anyone else get in?"

"Ah... because another bus just came and everyone at the station took it. However, you and I are so lucky and we found an empty microbus with AC and curtains."

"Yeah."

Mido rested his head on the back of the seat and fell asleep. When he woke up, he found himself lying somewhere he didn't know. Mido freaked out, got up, and ran to look for a door. He pulled on the door, but it didn't open. Mido's eyes teared up out of fear. And then he heard a voice from the other side of the door. Mido brought a chair over and looked through the keyhole in the door. He saw the woman who was on the bus, the driver, and the man who was standing by the door of the bus. The chair he was standing on wobbled and he almost fell.

"Did you hear that?" the driver asked.

"No, is there something wrong?" the second man replied.

"Maybe the boy woke up," answered the woman.

"Let me go and check," said the man.

ميدو اوّل ما سِمع خطَواتْهُم جِرى بِسُرْعه و اِستخبّى تحْت السَّرير. الباب اِتْفتح و الرّاجِل لمّا لقاه مِش علىَ السَّرير نادى علىَ صُحابُه.
—الحقوا! ده مِش مَوْجود فى الاوْضه!
—يَعْنى ايه مِش مَوْجود! الباب كان مقْفول بالمِفْتاح و اِحْنا فى الدّوْر الخامِس. دوّر كُوَيِّس! قالِت السِّتّ.

بدأوا يدوّروا فى الدّولاب و وَرا السّتايِر، و بدأ ميدو يِتْسِحِب واحْده واحْده و طِلِع مِن تحْت السَّرير. وقِف وَرا الباب و بعْديْن اوَّل ما لقاهُم مشْغولين طِلِع يِجْرى جامِد بعْديْن مِن الخوْف اِتْكعْبِل و وِقِع علىَ الارْض.

—ايْه الصَّوْت ده!
—ده بايْنُه هُوَّ الواد، ردّ السِّوّاق.
—بِسُرْعه! قالِت السِّتّ.

طِلْعوا يِجْروا بسّ ميدو كان قام جِرى و اِسْتخبّى فى اوْضه لقاها.

—مِش مَوْجود برّه!
—يَعْنى ايه؟ **فصّ مِلْح و داب!** دوّروا كُوَيِّس عليْه! هِىَّ الشّقّه كُلّها كام اوْضه؟
—طيِّب طيِّب، انا هدوّر عليْه فى المطْبخ و حدّ يِروح يِشوفُه فى الحمام و حدّ ميتحرَّكْش مِن هِنا لحْسن يطْلع يِجْرى و يِسهِّينا.
—تمام! قال الرّاجْليْن فى نفْس الوَقْت.

When Mido heard their steps, he ran quickly and hid under the bed. The door opened, and when the man didn't find him on the bed, he called his friends.

"Hey look! He's not in the room!"

"What do you mean he's not there? The door was locked and we're on the fifth floor. Look around good!" said the woman.

They started looking in the wardrobe and behind the curtains. Mido started to sneak little by little out from under the bed. He stood behind the door, and as soon as they were busy, he then ran quickly out of fear, stumbled, and fell on the floor.

"What was that sound?"

"It sounds like the kid!" the driver replied.

"Quick!" said the woman.

They took off running, but Mido had gotten up and hidden in a room he found.

"He's not outside!"

"What does that mean? He just vanished into thin air? Look for him good! How many rooms are there in the apartment anyway?!"

"Okay, okay! I'll look for him in the kitchen, and someone go look in the bathroom, and someone don't move from here, or else he might run off without us noticing."

"All right!" the two men said at the same time.

فصّ ملْح و داب (lit. *a grain of salt and it dissolves*) *vanishes into thin air*

ميدو فِضِل قاعِد خايِف جِدّاً و مِش عارِف يِعْمِل ايه. فِضِل يِحِسِّس فى الضِّلمه لقَى حوْض و عِرِف إنُّه فى الحمّام و السِّت جايّالُه. حسِّس حَوالِيْه و لقَى بانْيو دخل فيه و قفل السِّتاره و قعد خايِف.

شُوَيّه و السِّت فتحِت النّور و ملقِتوش. نادِت بِصوْت عالى: "مِش فى الحمّام! لقيْتُه عنْدك يا حمْدى؟"

—لا مفيش حدّ هِنا فى المطْبخ، ردّ السِّوّاق.
—ما تِدوّروا كُوَيِّس يا امّا حدّ فيكو بِيجى يُقِف هِنا جنْب باب الشِّقّه و انا هدوّر بِنفْسى! قال الرّاجِل التّانى.

طِلعِت السِّت و قفلِت نور الحمّام و وِقْفِت جنْب الباب مِسْتنّيه تِشوف لوْ سعيد (الرّاجِل التّانى) لقَى حاجه.

خرج ميدو مِن البانْيو و وِقِف جنْب الباب يِبُصّ. اوّل ما دخل سعيد المطْبخ طِلِع يِجْرى ناحْيِة باب الشِّقّه. ميدو لقَى السِّت واقْفه عنْد الباب بِالظّبْط.

—ها لقيْت حاجه؟ السِّت نادِت.
—اِسْكُتى شُوَيّه! ردّ الرّاجِل بِغضب.

سِمِع ميدو خطَوات الرّاجِل بِتْقرّب. راح طلّع مِن جيْبُه اسْتيكه كان حاطِطْها معاه و رماها بِاقْوَى حاجه عنْدُه. راحِت خبطِت فى فازه وَقِّعِتْها.

Mido sat very scared, having no idea what to do. He reached around in the dark and found a sink, and he knew that he was in a bathroom and that the woman was coming for him. He felt around and found a bathtub, got in it, closed the curtain, and sat in fear.

A few moments later, the woman came and switched on the light but didn't find him. She loudly called out, "He isn't in the bathroom! Did you find him, Hamdi?"

"No! There's no one here in the kitchen," answered the driver.

"Look around good! Or, one of you, come here and stand by the door of the apartment and I'll search myself," said the second man.

The woman went out and switched off the light, and stood by the door waiting to see if Sa'eed (the other man) had found anything.

Mido got out of the tub and stood by the door, looking. Once Sa'eed entered the kitchen, he ran toward the door of the apartment. Mido found the woman standing right by the door.

"Hey, did you find anything?" the woman called.

"Shut up for a bit!" the man answered angrily.

Mido heard the man's steps approaching. He took an eraser that he'd taken with him out of his pocket and threw it as hard as he could. It hit a vase and made it fall.

جِرْيوا كُلُّهُم ناحْيةِ الصّوْت و راح ميدو طِلع مِن الزّاوْيَه اللى كان مِسْتخبّى فيها و فتح الباب و نِزِل بِسُرْعه يِجْرى.

"بُصّوا! باب الشَّقّه اِتْفتح!" صرخِت السِّتّ: "بِسُرْعه وَراه!"

فتحوا الباب بصّوا مِن بير السِّلِّم لقوه نازِل.

"اهو لِسّه بِيْنزِل! بِسُرْعه بِسُرْعه!"

نِزِل الرّاجْليْن يِجروا وَراه و بعْديْن و ميدو نازِل بِسُرْعه باب شقّه اِتْفتح و سِتّ كِبيره بصّت لِميدو و سأَلِتُه: "بِتِجْرى ليْه كِده يا حبيبى. اِوْعَى لَتُقَع."

حاوِل ميدو يرُدّ عليْها بسّ صوْتُه مطْلِعْش. قبْل ما يِلْحق يِكمِّل جِرى الرّاجْليْن وِصْلوله و مِسْكوه. فِضِل ميدو يحاوِل يِصوّت يِصوّت مِش عارِف برْضُه.

بصّ لِلسِّتّ العجوزه و مدّ اِيدُه فى اِسْتِغاثه. راحِت السِّتّ مِسْكِتُه مِن اِيدْهُم و قالِت: "اِصْحَى يا ميدو..اِصْحَى!"

They all ran toward the sound. And Mido got out of the corner where he was hiding, opened the door, and ran out quickly.

"Look! The apartment door is open!" the woman shouted. "Quick! Go after him!"

They opened the door and looked down the stairwell and saw him going down.

"That's him! He's still on the stairs. Quick, quick!"

The two men went down after him. Then, as Mido was going down, the door of an apartment opened and an old woman looked at Mido and asked him, "Why are you running, honey? Watch out so you don't fall."

Mido tried to answer her, but no sound came out. Before he could continue running, the two men reached him and caught him. Mido kept trying to scream and scream, but he couldn't, either.

He looked at the old woman and held his hand out in a bid for help. The old woman held his hand and said, "Wake up, Mido! Wake up!"

اِوْعَى لَتُقَّع *Beware lest you fall!* The prefix لَ is synonymous with لحْسن and is not to be confused with the prefix لِ *to.*

فتح ميدو عيْنُه لقَى مامْتُه هِيَّ اللى بِتْناديه عشان يِصْحَى.
—ماما! قال و هُوَّ لِسَّه مخْضوض.
—اِنْتَ ايْه بسّ اللى نيِّمك علَى الكنبه كِده؟ قوم نام علَى سريرك. و كِده سِبْت التِّلِفِزْيوْن مفْتوح؟ و ايْه ده كمان اللى اِنْتَ بِتِتْفرّج عليْه ده؟ مِش قُلْنا بلاش الافْلام العنيفه دى؟

بصّ ميدو علَى التِّلِفِزْيوْن و لقَى عصابه بِتْطارِد واحِد بِمُسدّسات.

ضِحِك ميدو و قال: "ها ها ها..عنْدِك حقّ و هسْمع كلامِك بعْد كِده يا ماما.."

Mido opened his eyes to find it was his mom who was calling out to him to wake up.

"Mom!" he said, still scared.

"What made you fall asleep on the couch like this? Get up and sleep in your bed. And why did you leave the TV on? And what is this you're watching? Haven't we said not to watch these violent movies?"

Mido looked at the TV and saw a gang with guns chasing a man.

Mido laughed and said, "You're right. I'll listen to you from now on, Mom."

lingualism

Visit our website for information on current and upcoming titles, free excerpts, and language learning resources.

www.lingualism.com

www.ingramcontent.com/pod-product-compliance
Lightning Source LLC
Chambersburg PA
CBHW020616300426
44113CB00007B/671